Design Your Fabulous Next Chapter

DESIGN YOUR FABULOUS NEXT CHAPTER

7 STEPS TO A LIFE WITH MORE JOY AND FULFILLMENT

SHARRI HARMEL

MAVISSEN MEDIA

BOSTON, MA, USA

Mavissen Media

Boston, MA, USA

Library of Congress Control Number 2024925051

Paperback ISBN: 979-8-9918083-0-9

eBook ISBN: 979-8-9918083-1-6

Book cover and interior design by Christina Thiele

Editorial production by KN Literary Arts

This book is dedicated to all the women who reach that pivotal moment in their lives when they ask, "There must be something more." To those ready to embark on the journey of transforming their deepest desires into reality: Your courage to change your own life will ripple out, positively impacting your families, communities, and ultimately the world.

To my children, Kelly and Jeremy, may you walk through life with the courage to embrace your true selves, always living with authenticity and integrity. May honesty be your guiding star as you speak and act with truth in both your brightest and darkest moments. May your hearts be filled with love, not only for others but also for yourselves, knowing that love has the power to heal and uplift.

And to my nine beautiful grandchildren, Lainey, Leia, Leo, Katie, Charlie, Isaac, Parker, Isabella, and James: You are the future. Remember that your values and sense of self will serve as your compass as you design your many next chapters.

I love you all.

Contents

Introduction

Congratulations, dear reader! If you're holding this book, chances are you are in the midst of a significant transition—whether you call it a reinvention, a pivot, or a major life change. You've chosen to face that transition head on, taking a pro-active approach to creating the next chapter of your life. That's a courageous decision, and it's the first step toward building a future that is truly yours.

You may find yourself at this crossroads for many reasons. Perhaps your children have grown and launched into adulthood, leaving you with an empty nest. Maybe you're navigating the end of a relationship or going through a divorce. It could be the looming prospect of retirement forcing you to restructure time once filled with a career you spent decades building. Or maybe your shift is more subtle—an inner whisper that something is missing, a longing for passion and purpose.

No matter what your personal circumstances are, these changes are significant. By picking up this book you've already taken a bold step toward taking the reins to design your next fabulous chapter. You're ready to move forward—and this book is here to guide you on that journey.

Let's dive in and embrace this exciting new phase of life together.

No matter what kind of transition you're dealing with right now, I understand, because I've been there too. While we all have unique life experiences, the challenges life throws at us are universal. I'll share parts of my personal story with you on this journey, hoping that you'll find comfort in knowing that if I've made it through some of my own significant transitions, so can you.

Transitions are hard. But we manage them better when we have support. My hope is that this book not only encourages self-reflection but also opens up meaningful conversations with others—whether that's close friends working through chapters together or connecting with like-minded women in a supportive community, like a Facebook group. If you want more personalized guidance, individual coaching is always an option as well.

My watershed year was 2010. It was the moment when everything I'd been juggling—whether by choice or circumstance—suddenly came into sharp focus, and I had to ask myself: "Who am I? What truly matters to me? Where is my life heading, and if I'm not the one steering it, who is?"

My journey, though, began long before that. At eighteen, I got pregnant by my high school boyfriend and made the heartbreaking decision to give my son up for adoption—a loss that became a permanent wound. Years later, when I chose to reconnect with my son, it set off a chain of events that led me to confront those crucial questions about life, identity, and purpose. That decision had many consequences in my life, but it was a gift that propelled me to ask those very important questions.

After high school, I went on to get a university degree and worked as a stockbroker back when there were precious few women in the financial services industry. I later fell in love with and married a man whom I kept thinking would one day wake up and realize how much he loved me back. Spoiler alert: He didn't. But I am nothing if not optimistic and hardworking, so

I kept trying to make the marriage work for twenty-five years! In that time, I raised a daughter who struggled with dyslexia and other learning differences. I poured myself into my role as my daughter's advocate, voice, and interpreter, as well as her mom. I also created a beautiful home for my family and used my business skills to help my husband build a very successful and lucrative career. I gave my imperfect life my very all, and I wouldn't go back and change any part of it. Those two-and-a-half decades taught me so much about myself, my family, my marriage, and the world of business. I focused on my strengths, one of which is tenacious loyalty, and I made the most of everything that came my way.

Sound familiar? I'm guessing it does, even if some of the details vary. We women get things done, don't we? We start out with dreams, and, of course, life comes along and throws hurdles our way. Very few of us get the ideal version of life we envisioned as teenagers. Yet, we learn, we grow, we adapt, and no one works harder than we do to build a good life for ourselves and those around us. We face the unexpected with resilience—sometimes because we have no choice, and other times because we recognize our own strengths. We pour ourselves into our families, our careers, and our communities, often juggling more than we ever imagined. Along the way, we learn to rely on our tenacity, our loyalty, and our unwavering ability to make the best of what life throws at us.

This book is a reflection of that journey—my journey—but it's also yours. It's about how we, as women, take life's imperfections and shape them into something beautiful. It's about the lessons we learn, the love we give, and the hard-earned wisdom that comes from living a life that may not have gone exactly as planned, but is deeply meaningful nonetheless. So, here's to us—to our strength, our perseverance, and our ability to thrive, no matter what.

My thinking and wondering began years before my watershed year. Something had slowly begun to stir inside me. My daughter became an adult, and I began to wonder what lay ahead for me beyond all the planning and doing of my busy everyday life. What was next? Could I look forward to any adventures, or was my life going to be one unending calendar of activities, events, and achievements so that I could I avoid feeling lonely? I knew I had to have the courage to make some big changes, none of which were easy. First, I set out to locate the son I had given up for adoption as a teenager. Then I entered graduate school to get a master's degree in counseling. Then I filed for divorce.

I don't have to tell you that reconnecting with my birth son, admiring both the family who raised him and the wonderful husband and father he'd grown into, was an incredible experience. (I'll share more about that later.) Unfortunately, it also triggered a reaction in my own parents due to the role they had played in my teenage pregnancy. Not able to face the exposure of what they had done versus the image they presented to the world, they took the easy route and cut me out of the family. Was that difficult and unforeseen? Yes. Had I known the outcome, would it have changed my decision? No. The loving relationship I now have with my son and those grandchildren has brought me happiness beyond my wildest dreams.

But that wasn't all. I finally filed for divorce, and that, too, turned out to be much harder than I ever expected. Years before, my husband and I had promised each other that, if the marriage ever ended, we would approach the situation with fairness and civility. But when the time came, all those promises crumbled. He fought me over the money as if he were a two-year-old child forced to share his favorite toy. Every discussion became a battle, every deposition was heartbreaking. What should have been a relatively straightforward process dragged on for over two years, ultimately culminating in a trial. It was exhausting—emotionally, financially, and mentally. A drawn-out end to something we once promised would never become bitter.

You've heard this story before. You may have even lived it yourself. During those two years I cried, I comfort-ate to the tune of fifty extra pounds, and I binged a whole lot of DVDs (those were the days). Looking back, I see every step was necessary in my process.

Meanwhile, I was deep into my master's final year with a practicum at the University of Central Florida. This is where the turning point came. The university hired me to work with pre-med students who were failing their coursework and precariously close to being expelled. These students were struggling to contribute financially to their families, raising their own children (or siblings) while attending school. Some international students were worried about regime changes in their war-torn native countries and the well-being of family back home. As I sat in my tiny office helping these young people navigate their way through college or reimagine a different career path, a flame was lit. I'd leave work and drive home to my apartment, bogged down with the emotions of a divorce and an estrangement from my family, but inspired by the young people I worked with each day. If the very brave young people I met with day after day could create successful lives, I could certainly recreate mine. If I could make a difference for them, I could also make a difference for myself. If I could coach them, I could coach me!

Finally, I made a promise to myself that I was going to feel happy again. No matter how long it took, I was determined to create a next chapter for myself, filled with things that brought me joy and surrounded by people who truly mattered. I became passionate about building a life where I could contribute meaningfully and be valued for who I am. It wasn't just about moving forward—it was about designing a home and a community that nurtured me and fed the creativity that had been reignited through my struggles. With every step, I rediscovered pieces of myself I had forgotten, and slowly, happiness began to feel possible again.

I finished my degree, reentered the work force, and moved to Boston, a city I had loved in the past, one that held no "couple memories" to haunt me. I bought an apartment and relished the freedom of decorating it entirely to my own taste. I tried to make new friends, determined to show the world (especially my ex-husband and my parents) that, despite being nearly destroyed by the long, brutal divorce and family abandonment, I could rise up and create a fulfilling life as a strong, middle-aged woman.

I'm not going to lie. I had many sleepless nights in Boston. I would wake up in the early hours of the morning, gripped by the fear of being alone, with no family or partner. My recurring nightmare was that I would run out of money and become a bag lady on the street pushing a grocery cart filled with all my belongings. I asked myself big terrifying questions about aging alone and the more mundane worries like the safety of walking home alone from the theater, how to fix a broken appliance, and dealing with repair people who could only come during working hours. Every little thing that I had once handled with ease suddenly felt complicated and scary.

But beneath the fear and loneliness, I felt a stirring of rest-lessness, a flicker of motivation that reminded me of the person I had once been. Deep down, I knew there had to be more to life, and I was on a mission to discover it. Armed with a journal, a handful of vision board materials, more self-help books than I could count, and the fierce determination to figure out my life before time ran out, I began walking through the seven-step process that would ultimately shape this book. I wrote this book not just for myself, but for you too.

Wherever you are right now—whether you're feeling the first stirrings of restlessness, preparing to reenter school or the work force, or binging on bad TV with popcorn for dinner in the midst of a heartbreak—this seven-step framework can guide you toward clarity. It's designed to help you figure out what you truly want and what it will take to get there. These are the same steps I took myself as I slowly built the fabulous next chapter of my life, the one I'm now living.

If I could rise from the ashes of my hardest days and create something beautiful, I believe you can too.

I now split my time between Paris and Boston, with regular visits to Minneapolis where my children and grandchildren live. My life is a balance of work and play, freedom and responsibility, and I cherish every moment of it. I work for myself, and I love what I do each and every day, creating content and coaching clients who are focused on designing and living their own fabu-lous next chapters. I have friends in cities across the globe, and I've built a strong, supportive community that keeps me inspired and connected. My relationships with my grown children and grandchildren are a top priority, and I devote meaningful time to nurturing those bonds. What excites me most is that I've reconnected to my dreams. I now shape my schedule around them, giving myself the freedom to pursue the things that set my soul on fire. I've embraced my feminine side again—allowing beauty, color, vibrancy, and passion to flow back into my life. I've even decided to brave the so-called final frontier of dating after sixty, which has been a whole adventure in itself!

Is my life perfect? No, of course not. But it is fully mine. I've crafted a life that feels like a true reflection of who I am—one that aligns with the vision and stirrings of my soul. It's engaging, fulfilling, and uniquely mine. And that's exactly what I want for you too. My journey shows that it's never too late to design the life you want, and I'm here to help guide you as you create your own next chapter—one that's rich with meaning, joy, and personal fulfillment.

———

A few final thoughts: As we dive into the seven-step process, it will be tempting to spend too much time looking in the rearview mirror. It's natural. There are more years behind us than ahead, and it's easy to wonder what might have been, or how things could have turned out if we'd made different choices. I understand. But creating a fabulous next chapter is about using the wisdom of our past and the lessons we've learned to shape the future we are building. Designing, planning, practicing, and living an incredible next chapter is one of the gifts of our generation. Never before have women had the opportunity to ask—after the kids have grown or the long career has ended—*what do I want?* We are the lucky ones! We just need a little encouragement and guidance along the way.

To get started, all you'll need is a journal, a pen, and the accompanying workbook you can download from my website via the QR code below. Make sure to pull out your journal and the online workbook for the activities that are part of each step. Resist the urge to jump ahead. Each chapter and step builds upon the previous one, so take it one step at a time.

Thank you for trusting me as your guide on this journey. Not only have I traveled this path myself, but I've also helped many clients along it as well. Now, you're my newest traveling partner. Let's get started on the road to *your* fabulous next chapter!

Step

Dream Big

The first step in designing your next chapter is to capture all your dreams about what the rest of your life could look like: the serious ones, the frivolous ones, and even a few wild and crazy ones. No editing and no boundaries. Let your imagination have free rein. If your life were a movie (and in some ways, it is), you'd be the writer, producer, director, and star. You get to make this movie exactly what you want, and the first step is to let your imagination out of its confines to do what it does best: envision.

My Story

A few months after my divorce became final, I signed up for a women's group tour to Paris hosted by the writer Jamie Cat Callan. She called it the Ooh La La Tour after her book, *Ooh La La!: French Women's Secrets to Feeling Beautiful Every Day.*

I wasn't expecting anything close to ooh-la-la at that point in my life, but the tour sounded like fun, and I badly needed a little fun. The tour was set for five days in July, and I even added on a few days before and after the tour so I'd have time to roam Paris alone.

Almost immediately upon arriving at my boutique hotel nestled between the 5th and 6th arrondissements, I noticed that life for Parisian women my age was different from that of women in America. Waiters actually looked me in the eyes when they asked if I would like to order the plat du jour. Instead of seating me at a table near the restroom, the maître d' at Le Hibou café would give me a choice window seat looking out to the busy street. Women in their fifties, sixties, and beyond dressed chicly in tailored slacks or flowy skirts, delicate blouses, and ubiquitous French scarves, even in summer. They wore kitten heels or ballet flats and tasteful, colored lipstick. They walked confidently down the street, greeted friends with standard double-cheek kisses, their body language relaxed and infused with the kind of enjoyment reserved only for young people back in the States.

These Parisiennes seemed to be an entirely different breed of woman. I was intrigued.

Every morning, I'd find myself on Le Hibou's outdoor terrace with my espresso and baguette with jam, watching Parisians rushing to work, parents with children, women with groceries, professionals riding bicycles in heels. A movie began to play in my mind where I was one of them—shopping, meeting friends, greeting others with a kiss on the cheek. In my movie, I was pretty and slim again and had an air of confident femininity. Little did I know at the time, these daydreams were the first step to creating a whole new life for myself.

After a week of roaming Paris alone, our tour began. One of the first places Jamie took us was La Maison Cadolle, one of the oldest couture lingerie ateliers in Paris, run by Poupie Cadolle and her daughter, Patricia. The atelier was unlike any shop I had ever visited. Thick pink carpet covered the floor, muffling all sound. We sat in chairs upholstered with velvets and animal prints and watched as Madame Cadolle extracted the most gorgeous lace and satin pieces from boxes nestled inside mirrored cabinets. And of course, there was champagne.

I sat perched on the edge of a loveseat, feeling incredibly uncomfortable with the sexiness of the energy inside the atelier.

Poupie Cadolle, who has since become one of my closest

friends, told a story I will never forget. A long-term customer was visiting the shop with her husband. The woman would go into the dressing room and try on a sample while her husband sat on one of the animal print chairs. When she emerged, she would model the piece for her husband as they discussed the fabric, color, and lace, and how each component complimented the woman's skin color. I could see them in my mind's eye. The exchange of opinions, the softness of the fabric between their fingers almost like a caress, the husband complimenting how beautiful each piece looked on his wife. When Poupie ended the story by revealing that this couple were both in their eighties, my eyes filled with tears that I quickly wiped away.

I wanted to be that woman. Who wouldn't?

Thankfully, Poupie switched topics and began describing the couture process, which includes multiple appointments so that each bra fit the woman's breasts just right. Cadolle is an incredible company all about women: not only the beautiful lingerie the company has created now for six generations, but also the women who run it. In 1889, Herminie Cadolle invented the very first bra by essentially cutting the corset in two in order to give women a more comfortable option. Today, Patricia is running Cadolle's along with her mother, Poupie Cadolle. This family of inspirational women and the beautiful artistry they had created made me feel as though I had fallen into a romantic novel. The presentation wrapped up and everyone started toward the door. I approached Poupie to thank her for her time, and before I realized what was coming out of my mouth, I asked for an appointment.

Poupie graciously said yes, and my appointment was scheduled for four days later.

I went back to our hotel, laid down on my bed, and sobbed. I didn't know why the lingerie experience had caused me to break down, but the emotions in me were undeniable, and I just let them flow. "Ugly cry" doesn't even begin to describe it.

That evening, we had a Seine River cruise planned. I splashed cold water on my swollen eyes and gently put on makeup to hide the blotches. I went downstairs to meet the group in the lobby, and we walked to the boat. On board, I found a seat as close to the water as possible. I felt raw and didn't want to speak with anyone.

Evening fell and the city lit up. Slumped in my seat, watching the charming scene float by, I started to tear up again, and this time the source of my grief became apparent. I would never have a true love in this lifetime. My chance to be adored and cherished like the woman in Poupie's story was nothing more than a fantasy. It was too late for me. Tears filled my eyes, blurring the twinkling lights of the city.

Suddenly, I heard a voice, loud and clear: "Sharri, you need to learn to love yourself, even if it's the only love affair you have in this lifetime. Your life will change if you learn to treat yourself as you want a lover to treat you."

I sat up, totally shocked. Had anyone else heard that? I looked around at the other women, then up at the bridge we were passing under. Suddenly it was as though my view had cleared, and light and goodness flowed in. I was in one of the most beautiful cities on Earth, floating down the Seine. All the magic and romance of Paris flooded into me. For the first time in many years, even decades, I felt surrounded by love.

I now call the voice I heard that night my Paris Angel.

A few days later, though, I walked to the atelier for my scheduled appointment with Madame Cadolle wondering what I had done. Getting fitted for a couture bra was so outside the box I had created for myself. What made me think I could be like all the women I saw walking up and down Rue Saint-Honoré—confident, relaxed, sensual? I was terrified knowing I'd have to show my breasts. It had been a long time since anyone other than myself had seen my girls.

I shouldn't have worried. Poupie, dressed in a conservative navy dress and jacket, her long blond hair pulled into a low chignon, warmly greeted me with a kiss on each cheek, and we began. She fitted me with a pattern her seamstress had created and began measuring, pinning, and re-pinning, all while chatting about her daughter and asking about my own children. Like all couture, multiple visits were required. That gave Poupie and me hours to discuss my divorce, her family, European history, French culture, and aging. In that atelier, I found a kindred spirit and a lifelong friend.

Thinking of my life back in Boston, I wondered why, in America, we women tended to save beautiful things only for special occasions that usually involved gaining the appreciation of others. Whether it is our fine china, handsewn tablecloths, designer outfits, or expensive lingerie, we rarely indulged in these luxuries without the participation of others. Wasn't our own appreciation enough?

The morning after the group tour was over, while sitting at one of my favorite cafés, I pulled out my journal and began writing down mental images of what my next chapter could look like: the way I wanted to feel, dress, earn money, socialize, and express myself in relationships. I found myself describing a new dream life in Paris, and my brain immediately chimed in: "This is crazy! You can't do this. It's too big, too scary, too wild. You cannot move to Paris."

I knew it was my analytical brain's job to think this way, always with safety and caution in mind, and always looking at the potential roadblocks it might have to solve if I made a big change. I didn't argue, but I also didn't let it stop me. I sat looking at my desires right there in black-and-white on the page and began to brainstorm all the possible ways it *could work.*

A week later, my journal was filled with ideas that thrilled and revitalized me—even if I didn't yet know how to make them real. I walked out of Cadolle's after my final fitting and realized I was already a different woman. Paris had changed me. Everything was lighter, more exciting, and in Technicolor. I had been feeling invisible, but it was a cloak of invisibility I had voluntarily put on and, therefore, I also had the power to take it off. It was time to shed my invisibility cloak—or maybe even burn it in the backyard.

I suddenly saw all kinds of options for my future. I decided that:

- Even if I found that wonderful man to adore me, I would first learn to adore myself.
- Even if I had to walk away from the big family house filled with memories of my marriage and family of over twenty years, I could find an apartment and turn it into my own little jewel box.
- Even if I had let myself relinquish every official corporate title, I could still step into my skillset and start a business.

I don't know why Paris healed me, I just know she did. I used to say that I liked the woman I was when I was in Paris. Now I *am* that woman, all the time, not just when in Paris but wherever I happen to be living or traveling. "Paris Sharri" is the real and authentic Sharri, and my Paris Angel is still with me.

Now It's Your Turn to Dream

Our dreams matter. They add spark, juice, and joy to our lives. And when we get our dreams on paper, something shifts. Working with our dreams on paper gives them time to germinate, gives us time to sift through them, and gives our analytical brain time to soften around the knee-jerk caution and what-ifs it is so good at.

You'll discover that when you put your dreams on paper, you'll begin to see entirely new possibilities. Rather than coasting through your next chapter in neutral, reacting to what everyone around you wants from you, you'll take control and design your own fabulous next chapter.

You're going to explore not just the safe dreams that won't disrupt anyone else's life, but also the big dreams, the audacious dreams, dreams you've possibly had for a very long time but never had the opportunity or the freedom to pursue. Now is your time!

Don't worry though; we're going to start slow with a few gentle exercises to get the juices flowing and our imaginations working. Let's dive in!

Activity 1: Name Your Role Models

Which people, famous or not, living or dead, do you admire most in the world? What is it about them that inspires you?

My list looks something like this:

- Auntie Mary. Throughout sadness and challenge, she finds joy, fun, and opportunities every single day. She is an optimistic, loving woman.

- Queen Elizabeth. She showed great courage in stepping into leadership when few women had done so, forging new pathways in a constantly changing world. She balanced her job with her femininity, her love of family with her devotion to her country. She was strong yet soft, a woman of deep faith and purpose.

- Martha Stewart. She accepts who she is and is vulnerable enough to admit her failures. She is incredibly hardworking, super smart, and always open to the next big idea.

- George Washington. He was a born leader and yet had no desire to create a legacy. He used his strengths for his work and purpose, all the while keeping his ego in check.

- Benjamin Franklin. He was a brilliant, flawed man who never stopped thinking and creating. He never quit or found himself "too old" to achieve something.

Now it's your turn. Who do you admire most and why?

As you look over your list, circle the *qualities* each person holds that you admire most. Realize those qualities are also within you.

Activity 2: Name Your Favorite Movie Characters

When we watch our favorite movies, we are in a sort of dreamland, embodying the characters we connect with and traveling with them through their journey. Which movies do you watch over and over? What is it about those characters that you find so inspiring?

Here are a few of mine:

- Meg Ryan's character in *You've Got Mail*
- Jennifer Lopez's character in *Second Chances*
- Diane Keaton's character in *Something's Gotta Give*
- Meryl Streep's character in *Out of Africa*
- And of course, Diane Lane's character in *Under the Tuscan Sun*

It's easy to see what my favorite characters have in common: These women have businesses or careers they love, they are each searching for something more in life, and many of them discover a new aspect of themselves along the way. All of them inspire me to do more, be more.

Now it's your turn. List your favorite movie characters and the traits you love about them.

Remember, you are the writer of the screenplay of your next chapter. You're also the director, the main character, and the star. If writing this list makes you want to rewatch one of your favorites, please do! Ask yourself if there are certain qualities your character is exhibiting that you feel connected to or want within yourself. Pay attention to what you are feeling as you watch your favorite character act in ways that inspire you.

Activity 3: Brainstorm

For this exercise, take out a big sheet of white paper along with some colored pens. You're going to keep adding to this sheet as you go through the book, so the bigger it is, the better!

Take a few deep breaths and begin to imagine yourself designing the next several years of your life to go exactly as you want. What do they look like? Write down all the words and phrases that come up for you. Don't worry about connecting any dots, just write! Here are some prompts to help get you started:

- What dreams did I have a child and teenager?
- What dreams have I had for a long time as an adult?
- What is the wildest dream I could imagine for my future?
- What would I do if anything was possible, if I had no limits, all the resources in the world, and a cheerleading squad that supported me 100 percent?
- In my ideal life, how do I want to feel as I move through my day? What specific activities do I see myself doing? Do I look different? Do I speak or move or dress differently?
- What's next in my life? A side business? Downsizing? Quitting my corporate job? Moving to the country/city? Living in a new state/country? New friends? Rekindling old friendships? A new partner? A better marriage with my current partner?
- What am I good at that I also enjoy? (You're not allowed to list things you're good at that you *don't* enjoy!)

No aspect of your life is off-limits in this brainstorming session. *Welcome in every single idea no matter how crazy it may sound.* Your white sheet will be covered with ideas, words, and scribbles. It'll all come together, I promise!

Brainstorming Hurdles to Watch Out For

Thinking too small: Initially, your brain may offer up safe, ordinary, logical ideas that only require tiny life changes, little tweaks like losing a few pounds or reading a new book. That's because our brains love the familiar and the comfortable. It doesn't naturally leap to big, bold dreams. Assure your brain this is just a playful exercise and dare it to dream a little bigger; encourage it to stretch! Imagine you're writing a movie—and no one wants to watch a boring movie, so make it thrilling!

Filtering: As you dream big, your brain will likely jump in with practical questions; "How will I ever achieve that?" or "What about my obligations, my responsibilities?" This is your brain trying to do what it does best: solve problems. But that's not what brainstorming is for. Right now you're just exploring possibilities. You'll have time later to figure out the how. Trust that the trying on and analyzing stage will come, but not yet! You'll have plenty of time later to analyze, tweak, reorganize, and plan—I promise!

Going blank: Sometimes women tell me, "I'm not creative," "I don't have much of an imagination," or "I can't picture a future." If that is you, I ask, Have you ever worried yourself sick about things like retirement, old age, losing money, or any of a hundred other worst-case scenarios? Of course you have! Those are dreams too—they just happen to be nightmares, but they are still the product of an active imagination! If your brain is creative enough to imagine the worst-case scenarios, it's also capable of envisioning the best.

Negative stories: Not surprisingly, this is the biggest hurdle to brainstorming. You might hear thoughts like: "You're not smart enough!" or "You're much too old for that!" Or perhaps: "My family will never go for this" or "I can't reach out to that person, she will think I'm nuts!"

These negative stories are just that—stories. Author Byron Katie beautifully asks us to challenge those thoughts by asking, "Is it true?" and "Can I absolutely know it is true?" Those two questions usually shake me up and can dismantle any limiting beliefs that hold me back.

Expect these hurdles to arise—they're a natural part of how the analytical mind works. But as you continue through this process, you'll find that your creative side begins to take over, and brainstorming will flow more freely.

Extra Credit: Host a Brainstorming Party

One of the best ways to inspire yourself and overcome your own brainstorming blocks is to gather a group of friends and do this exercise together. When you share your ideas in a group, you gain the benefit of different perspectives, experiences, and talents. We often find it easier to spot strengths and opportunities in others than in ourselves, so this collaborative environment can be a real eye-opener. Not only does it make brainstorming more fun, but it also brings a fresh energy that can spark even more ideas. There's power in numbers; so invite your friends, make it social, and see what new possibilities emerge!

Activity 4: Keep a Dream Journal

We all dream when we sleep. The trick is to remember our dreams. Our subconscious mind communicates through dreams, offering clues to challenges we're facing, relationships we desire, or the kind of life we want. Dreams may hold insights and solutions or reveal things we haven't consciously realized.

I had a vivid dream about eight years before I left my husband. In the dream, my husband and I were climbing the pyramids in Egypt, which was unusual since we rarely traveled outside the United States. Before this dream, my husband had given me a beautiful Louis Vuitton purse, the nicest gift he'd ever given me. I adored that purse—it represented elegance to me, and I loved how everything fit inside. Even when I wore casual clothes, carrying that purse made me feel put together.

In the dream, as we climbed the pyramid, my husband was far ahead, yelling at me to keep up. I was struggling to climb, mostly because I was also hauling up the purse. Every few steps, I had to carefully reach down and bring it up, which slowed me down. My husband grew furious, shouting at me to leave the purse behind. But I couldn't. It was too important to me.

When I woke up, I was intrigued and wrote everything down. I later brought the dream to my therapist, who was skilled in dream analysis. We talked about whether the purse represented my materialism, wondering whether I was so attached to this luxury item that I was willing to risk my safety and my relationship. My therapist offered a different interpretation. The purse symbolized my true self, the part of me I couldn't abandon no matter how much my husband wanted me to. In my dream, I was being forced to choose between my marriage and my authentic self.

Throughout my marriage, I often had reoccurring dreams where I was in distress: surrounded by loved ones yet unable to warn them of an impending danger because I couldn't make a sound. I would try to scream but nothing came out. After my divorce, those dreams began to shift. Now, a decade later, my dreams, though still vivid, are dramatically different. No more dreams of struggling to keep up, being trapped in danger, or hanging from the edges of buildings.

Our dreams can deliver powerful messages about what we really need and what we need to change in order to get it.

For this exercise, keep a journal and pen near your bed. If you wake up from a dream, jot down whatever you can remember. Doing so will trigger your subconscious memories when you are fully awake. After a few weeks of this, try answering the following questions:

- What images, themes or patterns emerge in my dreams?
- Do any symbols or objects stand out? What might they represent to me?
- How do my dreams make me feel? Hopeful, anxious or something else?
- Have my dreams changed over time? If so, what might that signify about my life's progression?

Dream journaling can offer you unique insight and guidance from your subconscious, helping you to better understand yourself and navigate life's challenges. If you feel safe to do so, present the dream to a therapist or good friends and see what they think your dream elements could mean.

Activity 5: Make the Connections

You've recalled some of your favorite movie characters and role models, recorded your dreams, and brainstormed—and maybe even held a brainstorming party. Now, as you review your dream journal, your brainstorming sheet, and these exercises, take a moment to notice what themes are beginning to emerge. What do you find appearing over and over?

- Which images seem to repeat?
- What emotions am I feeling when I revisit my entries?
- Are there certain places or locations that show up more than once?
- What skills or activities are frequently mentioned?

We'll be using those recurring themes as you continue through this book. For now, you are priming your brain, teaching it what to focus on as you explore the elements of your next-chapter life.

Keep these reflections in mind. They are clues guiding you toward the future you're shaping for yourself.

Optional Woo-Woo Activity: Program Your Sleep Dreams

One of the most creative times in our day is during REM sleep, that final sleep cycle just before waking up. It's when our brain starts making the kinds of connections we can't always access in our waking hours. Many people have shared how they went to bed stuck on a problem, only to wake up with fresh ideas or solutions that came to them in their sleep.

Why not give this a try? After all the brainstorming and dream recording you've done, you already have a sense of what you want and how you want to feel. You probably also have a lot of thoughts about what's holding you back or making you feel stuck. Before going to bed tonight, write it all out in your dream journal: what you want, how you feel, what's blocking you. Then ask the universe, God, your angels—whatever you consider your higher power—for guidance.

Ask them to show you your next chapter in your dreams. Visualize yourself in the middle of that fantastic vision, engaged in activities you desire, feeling the emotions you want, and living the life you've been dreaming of. Ask to see if there is something more you've overlooked, and request that it be brought to your attention in your dreams.

Sweet dreams.

Step

2

Identify What Truly Matters

Midlife is a curious time. Inside, parts of us feel like we're eighteen years old again, and the possibilities are endless. Yet, when we look in the mirror we see the lines of our experiences, the weight of our babies gathering around our midsections, and the losses we've felt reflected in our eyes. All the ages and stages of our lives, the lessons and wisdom gained, are inside us. Yet, we still carry some of those youthful dreams—or maybe new dreams have been born.

Sometimes we pause and wonder how many years we have left to realize them. Arriving at age fifty-three, I suddenly found the space to ask: *What do I really want?* That question lingered in the air, heavy with possibilities and tough decisions.

Midlife may be the first time in many years, even decades, that you actually have the freedom to reflect upon and explore your own dreams. After my divorce, as I shared, I went on a women's trip to Paris and allowed myself to reflect on what life could still hold. Observing Parisian women who carried themselves with such elegance and confidence, I realized that this stage of life could be one of rediscovery, not decline. I saw how women my age in France were treated with respect, and it inspired me to believe it's never too late to reimagine life. So now is the perfect time to wonder: *What do I really want? And how do I make those dreams happen?* Midlife, with all its experiences and wisdom, offers us a newfound freedom—a chance to reshape our lives with the clarity that only comes after living through so many seasons.

My Story

We all have those moments when our lives take a detour that sets us on a new path. My first such experience happened in seventh grade. My father got into an argument with the head nun at my little Catholic school. One day I came home from school, oblivious to what had happened, and my mother told me I'd be attending the large public junior high *the very next day*.

St. Thomas the Apostle was the only school I had ever attended. I knew all the students as well as their siblings. My sixth-grade brother attended with me (he would now be sent to a public elementary school), and now, I was going to be the new kid entering in the middle of the school year at the local junior high. To top it off, I had never worn real outfits to school; my only morning dilemma had been whether I had a clean uniform to wear. To a seventh-grade girl, changing schools was terrifying.

I arrived at the school in a mental fog. I was used to being an A student and a good athlete, viewed as a leader. Suddenly I was invisible to both teachers and students, just one of the hundreds of kids in the hallways and classrooms.

The junior high spanned seventh through ninth grade. To me, the boys appeared to be men, and the girls all knew how to dress, some appearing much older than their years. There were cliques and groups galore, and each was a mystery to me.

But in my second week, a vivacious girl named Judie befriended me. Why, I have no idea. She was a smart, popular, lovely girl who immediately looped me into her circle of friends, many of whom came from successful Jewish families.

My world immediately expanded. I was invited into beautifully decorated homes, met mothers with careers and hired help. They wore dresses, nylons, and pretty shoes, while my mother lived in old jeans and baggy T-shirts. Fathers wore suits and carried briefcases, unlike my dad, who came home in work pants splattered with plaster. What struck me most was how these families interacted. They talked about education, grades, and university degrees, which were expected. It was clear, even to a seventh grader, that these families valued success in ways I'd never known.

At home, things couldn't have been more different. My mother, overwhelmed with five children, loved cleaning but hated cooking. We ate hotdogs, canned beans, and mystery casseroles. Understandably, she was exhausted. I always felt she would have been happier with one child and a job in a high-end women's clothing store. Instead, she lived in a house filled with hand-me-downs. She rarely left because she had no money to buy the beautiful clothing she loved and nowhere to go.

My father had met my mother and got a job as a plasterer because he lived in the house next door to her. Her father had a small plastering company. My mom was pretty, and he instantly became part of her family. Orphaned as a teenager, my father harbored deep frustrations about his lot in life. Though he was good-looking and could be funny and charming at times, underneath that facade he was angry, self-centered, and manipulative. He drank too much and, like his father, believed it was acceptable to hit and belittle his children when he felt provoked.

Neither of my parents had any formal education beyond high school, and while that wasn't unusual for their time, they didn't value learning.

I never told my new friends that I had no time or place to study and do homework or that my home was filled with angry putdowns and physical beatings. To afford clothing, I began working in a grocery store a distance away, and I kept this fact from my friends as well. I also never shared with my parents or siblings the cultural richness I experienced at my friends' homes or the deep respect I developed for Jewish traditions. I kept my two worlds separate.

In tenth grade, I fell in love with Jon, a Jewish boy who became my best friend. I loved him with the fierceness of first love, and by my senior year I got pregnant. All my dreams collapsed when our plans to marry were quashed by his wealthy parents, and mine were horrified by the shame. I was placed in an apartment in a desolate area, alone for six months, and pressured to give the baby up for adoption. My parents threatened to leave me on the streets if I didn't comply, and I believed them.

The isolation during my pregnancy created a pattern in me of ignoring my own desires. Once I gave the baby up, the only question in my mind was, "How can I earn back my parents' respect?" I focused on making choices that would impress them. I graduated from college, became a stockbroker (a career my father admired), and eventually married a successful corporate man. But my husband's success masked his inability to love and his dysfunctional relationship with his children from a previous marriage. I knew the signs of emotional unavailability, but after years of chasing love, he felt familiar and safe.

———

Our true selves, though, can't stay buried forever. Slowly, I reopened my box of dreams. I left my husband several times but always returned when he promised things would change. Nothing did, and after twenty years, I finally gathered the courage to ask myself: "Is this enough?" If things continued as they were, would I face my death filled with regret or feel satisfied for having followed my heart?

The answers were clear. It was lonelier to be in a loveless marriage than to live alone, and I wanted to find my son. I had no idea those two decisions would create such upheaval in my life, but I knew I had to make changes in my life to ever be truly happy.

I found my son, who had been adopted by a loving couple. He is a confident, loving, and successful man, father, and husband. I kept our relationship a secret for nine months, cherishing our budding friendship, and then I filed for divorce. When I told my parents I had found my son I expected them to be joyful, but they responded with anger and cruelty. They gave me a choice once again: my parents and siblings or my son. This time, I chose my son—and myself.

Those years were the hardest of my life. My ex-husband maligned me publicly, and my parents disowned me. But through it all, I felt a deep sense of peace. I had finally listened to my heart, and that painful journey paved the way for this next chapter of my life—and this book.

I share my story not for sympathy, but as an example of the struggles we all face when trying to honor our dreams. It begins with asking yourself: "What do I really want?" And that, my friends, is when the fun begins.

Time to Discover What Truly Matters to You

The next step in designing your fabulous next chapter is figuring out what is important to you *right now*. What do you truly value? What matters most to you? Those answers will guide you as you design a future that excites you. Your desires and values act like a compass or the GPS on your phone—they keep you headed in the direction you want to go.

There are two ways to approach this big question. First, there is the big picture, which might sound something like this: I want to travel, have adventures, maybe start a business, bring romance into my life, feel feminine again, and take care of the face and body I now have.

Sounds fantastic, right? But how are you going to make all that happen? Without a workable plan, our dreams and goals have a way of slipping to the bottom of our priority list. That's just human nature. We all get busy and tend to procrastinate on creating new habits that will bring us joy but sometimes require difficult changes. Also, even at our age, many of us still think we have loads of time to work on our dreams in some distant future. Humans are naturally optimistic, and optimism is lovely. But sometimes, unquestioning optimism doesn't serve us, and midlife is one of those times.

Time is limited and marches on regardless of how we use it. None of us wants to reach the end of life having ignored our most cherished dreams, always putting them off for "someday." Coasting through life doesn't bring lasting happiness. But don't worry—I'm not going to let you do that!

So, let's get started. First, we'll break down your big vision and focus on the specific timeframe of one year. Put on your one-year glasses and get ready to figure out what matters most to you for the next 365 days.

Activity 1: The Next Chapter Card Deck

I created the Next Chapter card deck to help you identify the most important points of your compass during this next year.

1. **First, download the cards here.**

Once you download the cards, print them and cut them out. Call me old school, but I want you to touch them, write on them, and connect to the feelings they bring, and that can't be done by staring at them on a screen.

2. **Go through the cards and on each one, write down what that category means to you.**

For example, for me the relationship card means getting out there and dating again. For another woman it might mean starting marital counseling. For a third it might mean getting engaged to a longtime partner. These are all very different interpretations. This work is personal, so you need to make it specific and aligned to your life right now.

A word of caution: Let go of any shoulds when you do your card deck. This is about what you want, so be on the lookout for the societal and cultural rules that tell us what a woman our age can and cannot do. They might sound like this:

- I *should* be available 24/7 for my adult children and grandchildren.
- I *should* move close to my children whether or not I like that city or town.
- I *must* have a significant other; I can't be alone.
- I *should* or *shouldn't* leave my current partner.
- I *should* own a home; renting is a waste of money.
- I *should* dress appropriately for my age.
- *I'm too old* to start a business, course of study, hobby, or relationship.

If you notice any of these shoulds creeping into your mind as you write on your cards, pause and let them go. This is about what you want, not what society says you should do.

As you write, really get in touch with the feelings you associate with each card's category, which is beyond what you'd actually achieve or create. For example, let's look at the creativity card:

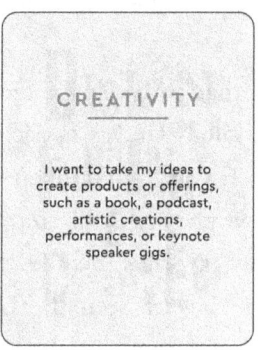

CREATIVITY

I want to take my ideas to create products or offerings, such as a book, a podcast, artistic creations, performances, or keynote speaker gigs.

This might be one definition of *creativity*.

Desired accomplishment: I want to take my ideas and create offerings, such as a book, a podcast, artistic creations, performances, or keynote speaker gigs.

Desired feelings: I want to feel I'm using my strengths to produce something that I'm proud of. I want to imagine myself setting aside time each day or week to dive into my creativity.

Another example. Say you define *creativity* as an artistic pursuit such as painting.

Desired accomplishment: I want to paint every day and produce enough paintings to be a part of an exhibit or a section in an art gallery.

Desired feeling: Every day I want to lean in to what it feels like when I am mixing colors, choosing a canvas, and applying brushstrokes.

Regardless of the card category, let yourself be enveloped by the feelings you want to feel and write it all down on the card.

When you connect to feelings, you allow your rational mind to calm down. Suddenly all those judgments and shoulds fall away, and it becomes easy to feel the feelings you desire in your next chapter.

Hot tip: One tip that always helps me connect to my feelings and quiet my rational mind is music. The power of music is incredible. It can shift your mood, open your heart, and spark creativity. As you move through this step, put on some uplifting tunes. Some of my favorites include "Don't Stop Believin'" by Journey and "You Haven't Seen the Last of Me" by Cher. Soundtracks can also ignite creativity. One of my favorites is the theme song for *Out of Africa* by John Barry. What are yours? Create your own playlist, let go of expectations, and allow yourself to be inspired as you explore each card!

3. Fill in any wild cards you need.

You'll notice that several of the cards are blank. These are your wild cards. They're for you to fill in any categories that are important to you that aren't already on the preprinted cards. For example, you might make a card labeled "Political Activism" or "Spiritual Development." Use as many wild cards as you need to make your deck fully represent you.

4. Make *yes* and *no* piles.

You've now got your stack of cards in front of you. Each card has your unique definition on it along with a description of the feelings you want to feel in that category. You may have added some wild cards. Now you are going to flip through one card at a time and decide which of the two piles it goes into.

One pile is *yes*. These are the desires and dreams you want to focus on in the coming year. (Remember, this isn't for life, just for one year!)

The other pile is *no*. These are the categories you feel you don't need to work on at all, perhaps because they are already solid. Or maybe they are categories you'd like to pursue sometime, but not right now.

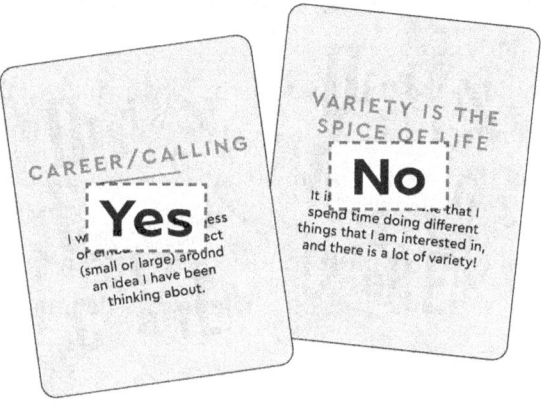

Put your no pile aside. Save them for another time.

5. Sort through your yes pile to find the top six.

Take the yes pile into your hand and lay out the first six cards on the table in front of you.

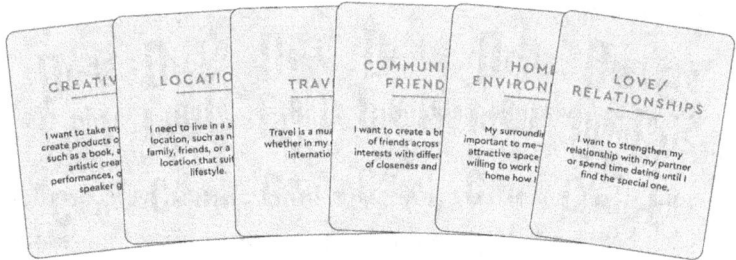

Now take the next card from the pile. Hold that card in your hand and ask yourself, *Is this category more important to me than any one of the six cards lying on the table?*

If yes, replace the card on the table with it. You can put the lesser important card either at the bottom of your yes deck or discard it into the no pile.

Go through the entire yes pile in this manner, taking one card at a time and checking to see if that category matters more to you than the six cards on the table. If it does, replace the less important card.

You will end up with six cards on the table in front of you. These six cards are the categories that matter the most to you as you design your next-chapter plan.

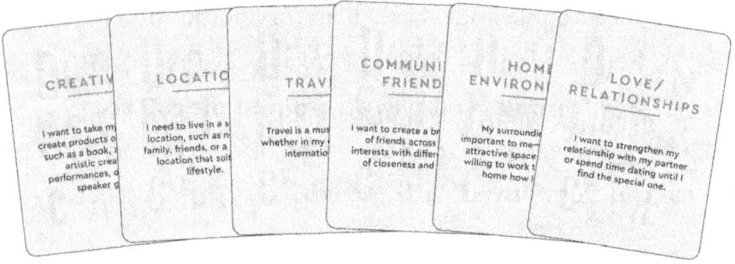

6. Rank your top six.

Next you will rank the six cards in order of importance. Obviously, all these categories are important to you or they wouldn't have ended up on the table. Use your intuition—don't overthink it—and simply rank them from 1 to 6. There is a reason you are ranking your card categories, which you'll discover in the next activity.

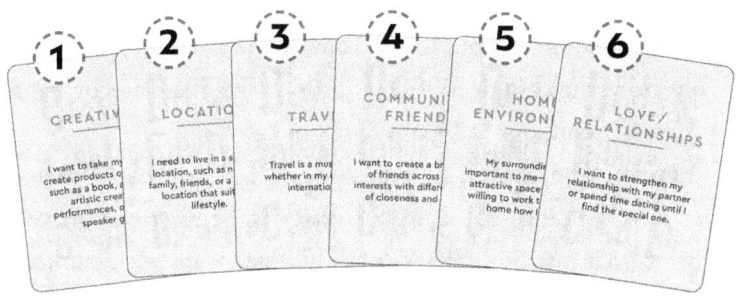

Activity 2: Your Vision Board

Let's talk vision boards.

Have you created vision boards filled with all sorts of photos and images, only to feel disappointed when none of it happens? Let's explore why that might be the case. What we typically do first is go through magazines, pulling out visuals that speak to us and then randomly glue them to a board. But without forethought or prioritization, you end up with a hodge-podge of visuals that don't have a clear focus.

Here's the key: For a vision board to work, you can't overload it with too much. Too many choices actually make us indecisive! How many nights have you lain awake with a multitude of ideas running through your head, yet you are unable to come up with a clear plan? You can't see what to do next, which is exactly why you toss and turn. That is what I call choice paralysis. Research backs this up. The more choices we face, the harder it is to move forward.

But fear not. I'm going to give you an entirely different way to create a vision board, and I promise you, it'll make the difference in what you accomplish this coming year.

1. Write in your top four categories.

Before you choose any photos, look at the six ranked cards you've set out from the card deck and write your top four categories on your vision board.

Most people choose four categories, but you can also use fewer if you prefer. Perhaps you really want to focus on two cards, or even just one. That's perfectly fine, as long as you keep it at no *more* than four categories. Create a section on your vision board for each category you want to focus on for the next year.

If it feels right, consider placing a reminder of your higher power in the center of the board. For me, that's an image of my angels; for you, it could be anything you define as a loving, higher power. It will look something like this:

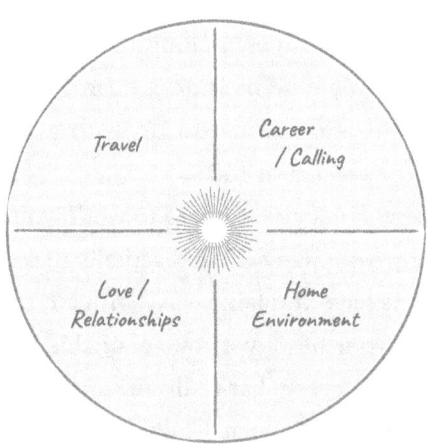

Note: As shown in the image, you can use lines to separate each category or omit the lines if you like.

2. **Breathe into the feelings of each category and choose photos to match.**

Focus on the categories you've written on your vision board. This is the important part: You can list the *things*, *events*, or *experiences* you want to achieve in that category, but spend more time focusing on the *feelings* you want to feel. You can choose to do this in your journal or on the cards themselves.

Now that you have identified the feelings you want to feel in each of these categories, start searching for images that match them. For instance, if your location card says, "I want to live near the ocean," and the feelings include "calm, grounded, connected to beauty," then keep those feelings in mind as you look at images. They might be images of the ocean, woodlands, clouds, whatever. Remind yourself to prioritize how the images make you feel.

Choose photos pertaining to your top four categories and remember to repeatedly ask yourself if the photos you're choosing evoke the feelings within you that you desire in each of the four categories. This step ensures that your board is truly aligned with your emotional goals.

Once you have your photos, plus any words that speak to you for each of your categories, glue everything in place. Remember, less is more. What is most important is that you can step into each of your categories and *feel how you want to feel* as you create the next year of your next chapter.

Once your board is finished, put it in a central, visible spot and take some time each day—preferably first thing in the morning—to look at it. Take in the images and words and recall the feelings you want to feel: who you want to be, how you want to interact with others, what you want to be doing. You are using the vision board to teach your mind and body to remember what you want in your next chapter. And as you do that, goodness will start appearing in your life.

I promise, this process will help you begin to recognize your truest feelings and desires for creating your next chapter.

Example: My Vision Board

I'm going to show you how I got beneath the surface of the categories to identify the feelings I wanted to have. My top four categories were:

- **Love/Relationships:** "I want to learn to enjoy dating."
- **Home Environment:** "I want to move to a different apartment in Boston and feel calmer by not having to do a total renovation."
- **Career/Calling:** "I want to continue to produce my YouTube podcasts and, more importantly, write my book!"
- **Travel:** "I want to continue to live part-time in Paris, visit friends, and see new places."

Let's start with love/relationships. When I got in touch with my feelings in this category, I realized that it'd been ten years since my divorce. Though I would like to find a soulmate at some point and though there are societal rules telling me I *should* find one as soon as possible, as I envisioned the feelings I wanted, I saw myself not getting married or settling down but going on dates. Yes, dates!

I wanted to feel brave, attractive, and able to have *fun* on dates. I wanted to feel interesting and engaged, maybe even flirty. It had been more than thirty-five years since I flirted with anyone other than my former husband. How fun would it be to meet a man for dinner and have a sparkling conversation? How fun would it be to dress up, smile at myself in the mirror, and walk out the door feeling confident? That's what I wanted.

On previous boards, I had photos of various dream soul-mates: a man with a successful career, a man with style like Cary Grant, a man who enjoyed travel and all the same things I do. Notice the difference between the focus on feelings and the way I approached previous vision boards.

Without connecting to the feelings I wanted, I didn't have any idea *how* that soulmate was going to arrive in my life. In my previous boards, the photos also showed solid, mature relationships—couples traveling the world, comfortable with each other, enjoying family time at home. But there was no leadup. It was comparable to signing up for a marathon without ever completing a 5K. I felt dating was a "waste of time," and those feelings created an outcome: I didn't go on any dates, and I obviously didn't find my soulmate.

This time, by connecting to the feelings I wanted to experience—fun, confidence, engagement, connection—I had to examine my must-have list for a soulmate and admit that:

- Maybe another CEO isn't going to give me these feelings (my former husband certainly didn't).
- Maybe physical attractiveness isn't my top priority, because attractiveness doesn't guarantee I'll feel any of my desired feelings.
- Maybe the men I date don't have to like everything I like. Maybe I can find joy and fun in opening up to new experiences.
- And last—this was profound for me—what trumps looks, success, financial achievement, and love of travel

is a man who has done his work. All of us must do the inner work to be capable of a loving, equal, fun, and caring relationship. A man who is present and responsible for his own well-being, rather than one dragging around a truckload of unresolved issues, is more likely to be someone I can feel confident, engaged, and able to have fun with!

Writing about feelings can help bust through all your "shoulds" and preconceptions.

Now let's look at the home environment category. My vision board said: "I want to move to a different apartment in Boston and feel calmer by not having to do a total renovation."

To do that, I'd first have to sell my condo. It required more renovation than I had the patience for. But I was also asking myself: *What is it with all my moving?* I'd been a nomad since my divorce, moving to another apartment every couple of years. Did I really need to move again, or should I suck it up and just get on with the renovation? I went back and forth on this to the point that I drove myself batty getting bids from so many contractors, I was sure they'd put me on their "do not answer" lists.

But then I connected to the *feelings* I wanted in my home environment: cozy, comfortable, elegant, and safe. Hmmm, safe. Why did that come up? Suddenly, I realized that I couldn't get excited to do the renovation because it didn't feel financially or emotionally safe. I knew from experience that renovations always cost at least twenty-five percent more than estimated, and I didn't want that much money wrapped up in my home. I also knew that as stressful as renovations could be, doing them as a single owner would be off-the-charts stressful.

As I journaled about all my previous moving, I realized I was seeking feelings that had nothing to do with my home. I had been chasing a certain type of community, pretty homes, and pretty locations. I was chasing new connections, new friends, and that old desire to feel I belonged somewhere. Journaling about the feelings and my vision board categories helped me understand what I was doing and what I really wanted.

It was only when I connected to my feelings that I realized that emotional and financial safety were a large part of my home dreams.

By identifying the feelings behind the desires, I got clear on what I really needed to do: sell the condo.

I hope this helps you understand how, once you have your categories set, journaling and diving deep into the feelings you want in each category will help you pull just the right images to place on your vision board. Have fun!

Congratulations on Finishing Your Vision Board

The vision board you've just created is an amazing tool to make your next-chapter dreams a reality. Imagine yourself already being the woman you aspire to be, experiencing all the feelings and moments you've envisioned. What's even more incredible is that you can repeat this process every year for the rest of your life, empowering yourself to become the creator of your future instead of coasting through life on autopilot.

On that note, each year writer Colette Baron-Reid offers an incredible free six-day vision board exercise. She's taught me everything I know and love about vision boards, so be sure to watch for her next offering!

Step

3

Get Clear on Where You Are Now

Bringing your attention back to the present moment right after creating a vision board might seem like backtracking. But, like any journey, identifying where you are right now is a crucial step. Just think of when you order an Uber. You know exactly where you want to go, and your driver also knows the destination. But if you don't know *where you are right now*, how will the driver find you? So, you look around, check out the street name, spot the nearest house address, and even check the direction of the traffic to determine what side of the street the car will find you on. Only when you've identified your correct, current location are you ready to begin your journey. It works the same when designing your next chapter!

My Story

I'm a future-oriented person. On every strength assessment I've ever taken, "futuristic" is my top strength. But sometimes that strength makes me so excited about what's ahead that I don't spend enough time figuring out where I am right now. I can imagine the future so vividly that I almost abandon the present.

Looking back, I realized that most of my decisions after my divorce—which city to live in, which apartment to purchase, which organizations or clubs to join, how to make new friends—were all based on me chasing happiness and connections.

Let's start with my first apartment purchase in Boston. Just a month after my divorce, I placed an offer on a two-bedroom apartment in an old brownstone on Marlborough Street. I had a vision for that apartment even before making the offer. The building had been fully renovated, converted into three apartments on five floors. Mine was on the third floor between two larger apartments below and above me. My neighbors were couples who had recently relocated from the West Coast after the husbands took high-level corporate jobs in Boston.

Before moving in, I imagined all the nice get-togethers I'd have with my new neighbors, complete with hors d'oeuvres, yummy wine, and maybe a dessert party I'd host in my apartment. Surely, I thought, building meetings would be harmonious with only three owners. My imagination carried me to a future I very much wanted.

However, once I moved in, the reality was quite different. The husbands were extremely busy and the wives were rarely home, and when they were, they were uninterested in my idealized gatherings. There were no cocktail or dinner invitations, and when I tried to connect to host a dessert party, it didn't work out. The building meetings? They were far from harmonious. I'd show up on time only to find the two wives had already been enjoying wine and nibbles before the meeting. With only three votes, mine mattered little. They hired and fired gardeners on a whim, each time adding new costs. After I moved in, I received nasty emails complaining that I laughed too loud, walked too hard (while waiting for my rugs to arrive), and that my car was too large, even though they each drove huge SUVs along with their husbands' sports cars. They even believed their cleaning ladies should be able to use my second parking spot because, as a single woman, I had no need for it.

I felt emotionally raw post-divorce and was sad that the future I had so beautifully imagined wasn't happening.

What did I do? Instead of assessing my current situation, I made a knee-jerk decision to sell my lovely apartment and buy into a new sixty-story, full-service building that promised a "community." My old neighborhood had been a quiet tree-lined street, whereas my new neighborhood was "in transition." Still, I convinced myself that even though the neighborhood was a little scary, the building's amenities—a restaurant, a fantastic gym, a spa, and package delivery—would solve all my problems. Plus, there were promised book clubs and lectures and presentations. It was going to be perfect. That's future-focused thinking!

I did love the full-service aspect of my new apartment, but in a building that large, true community is elusive. I ended up befriending the staff. At my first building party, I realized that most of the men my age were accompanied by women my daughter's age. Talk about feeling invisible!

The apartment's layout didn't fit my lifestyle either. It had a stunning living room with an incredible view, but the open kitchen had minimal countertops made of easily stained marble—completely impractical for an enthusiastic and messy cook like myself. The space was more suited to drinks before going out for dinner. I had bought an apartment in a high-rise designed for people who lived very differently from me.

If I had slowed down and analyzed what was wrong with my Marlborough Street brownstone, I might have found a way to fill the emotional hole inside me without moving. Instead, I made another impulsive decision and ended up moving three more times. Yes, I'm a slow learner! I was chasing happiness and community, and when I didn't find it, I kept moving to the next place.

I even continued this chase for happiness when I started

living part-time in Paris. After making friends with an American expat who lived in the 16th arrondissement, I impulsively started looking at apartment near her. I didn't stop to ask myself if the 16th, an area known for being quiet and expensive, was the right neighborhood for a single, older American woman who didn't speak French. My friend's life situation was entirely different from mine, but that didn't slow me down for one second. I was too excited about living near my new friend to ask myself those questions.

I put in an offer on a beautiful apartment near Rue de Passy, close to my new friend. It was huge, with a grand reception room, a small renovated eat-in kitchen, and two quiet bedrooms. I imagined all my decorating ideas in place, dinner parties, and my son and his wife coming to visit. I loved the quiet private bedrooms. The second bedroom, which would be my office, did seem very dark, but I was so taken by the fabulous living room and the proximity to my friend that I didn't question a thing. Again, I was chasing a feeling. I am a dream chaser.

Thankfully, the offer fell through due to paperwork discrepancies on the part of the seller that are too tedious to go into here. During the process, my French attorney advised me to end negotiations with the seller, and he also added that he thought the 16th arrondissement was not the right neighborhood for me. Luck intervened.

Later, I found an apartment I learned of through an acquaintance that was in the 7th arrondissement, closer to the places I loved such as Bon Marché, the Musée d'Orsay, and the Jardin des Tuileries.

Meanwhile, back in the States, a year before the COVID pandemic, both my children's marriages fell apart. Instead of visiting to support them, I felt I needed to move back to Minnesota to be near them. (Yep, I also have a hero complex.) So, I sold my apartment in that sixty-story, glass-enclosed building in Boston and bought a large historic home that needed a complete renovation but was close to both my kids. I had convinced myself that I needed the space for those big family gatherings I'd be hosting. I even dreamed I'd become a gardener, a new version of Martha Stewart. The renovation was incredibly time consuming and expensive, but I was going to be the matriarch I was born to be, finally!

Before the yearlong renovations were complete, both my kids found new partners and moved a good distance away. Looking back, it's almost laughable. I hadn't lived in Minnesota for almost fifteen years, and I hadn't lived in a single-family home for over seven, but I was determined to drive over every red flag until every reason for moving to Minnesota had changed.

This time, though, instead of impulsively moving again, I first explored Minneapolis, joined organizations and a church, reconnected with former friends, found doctors, and went to neighborhood gatherings. I shoveled the snow, rolled out the garbage can, and engaged with my kids and grandkids as often as they wished.

Then COVID hit. I finally slowed down and asked myself, "Where am I now? What am I doing?" By taking time to assess my present, I stopped chasing dreams and began making decisions based on my current needs. I realized I was lonely. Doing all that, deeply exploring *where I was*, helped me to finally make a sound decision that returning to Boston was the right choice for my next chapter. Acknowledging that I had been making impulsive decisions due to mindlessly chasing happiness and connection, I realized that Boston made more sense for me: Its size, multiculturalism, lifestyle offerings, and the directness of the people all agreed with my own temperament and needs. That made my next-chapter journey much clearer.

Sometimes we make new chapter plans in the midst of major life changes—divorces, new careers, menopause, becoming grandparents, problems our children may have, or even pandemics. The ground shifts, and our emotions can override common sense. That is why I've included this step in your next-chapter framework. Stop, take your time, and get really clear on where you are, because sometimes what you *think* you need, what you think will make everything right, isn't actually aligned with the next chapter you want.

So, Where Are You Now?

You've started designing your next chapter. You've worked through the Next Chapter card deck, prioritized your most important categories, and highlighted them on your new vision board with pictures that reflect the feelings you want to experience in those categories.

Isn't it wonderful to see your next-chapter feelings so perfectly displayed on your vision board? As you emotionally step into each category, you can feel exactly how you want to feel, as if you're already living that category in your next-chapter life.

You now have clarity around where you want to go. Wouldn't it be wonderful if you could wave a magic wand and make it all happen instantly? Unfortunately, it doesn't work that way. First, you need to identify where you are right now, *today*, in these most important areas of your life. Have your journal and your vision board nearby as you go through the following exercises.

Activity 1: Remind Yourself Where You Want to Go

Let's start with your vision board categories. They might look something like this:

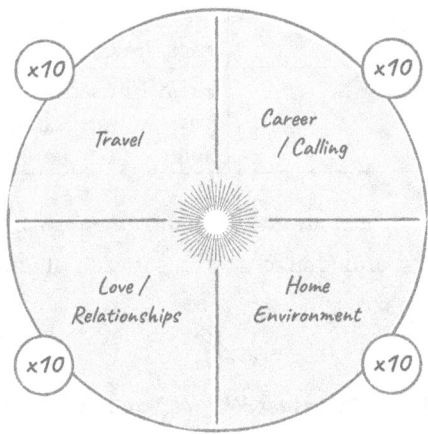

Start by listing your four categories (it's okay if you have fewer) in a circle, as in the above example. Next, add in how you know you want to feel in each of those categories a year from now, on a scale of 0 to 10. I wanted to feel a 10 in each, so I put 10 on the outside edge of each category.

Here is an example of my home environment category. You can see I added my feelings and then created summary characteristics of those desired feelings:

Characteristics	Feelings I want to feel . . .
Safe street/neighborhood	Safe in my home (day or night).
Secure package delivery area	I don't have to worry about theft of my deliveries.
Welcoming staff and building residents	I am a part of a family of sorts.
Beautiful architecture, furnishings	I am surrounded by beauty, which inspires my creativity.
A cook's kitchen with enough counter and storage space	I have a kitchen that's easy to work in, entertain in, and maybe even film in.
Affordable	Financially secure, no big surprises to worry about with my home.

Now, in your journal, go through this same process and list your own feelings and characteristics for each of your categories.

Activity 2: Assess Where You Are Today

Now, you're going to take those same vision board categories and rate yourself based on where you are *today* on a scale of 0 to 10. A zero means that you haven't successfully worked on this category for a good while, and a 10 means you've got it perfected (although the category probably wouldn't be on your vision board in the first place if it's exactly how you want it!).

How do you come to a rating for each of those categories? As an example, let's take a look at my home category again. I took that same chart and added the section of where I am today.

Characteristics	In my next chapter I want to feel . . .	Today I feel . . .
Safe street/ neighborhood	Safe in my home (day or night).	Safe in current location, although a little quiet at night.
Secure package delivery area	I don't have to worry about theft of my deliveries.	I don't have to worry about deliveries being stolen.
Welcoming staff and building residents	I am a part of a family of sorts.	The staff is very welcoming, but the residents are cold.
Beautiful architecture, furnishings	I am surrounded by beauty, which inspires my creativity.	Not at all surrounded by beauty. There is no architectural interest. I have to add and subtract to get close to pretty.
A cook's kitchen with enough counter and storage space	I have a kitchen that is easy to work in, entertain in, and maybe even film in.	Awful in my kitchen. There is no cupboard space, everything is falling apart, and there are nasty, thirty-year-old appliances.
Affordable	Financially secure, no big surprises to worry about with my home.	Stressed. The renovation will cost significantly more money, time, and energy than I have. Nothing of quality was previously done in this apartment.

You can see I already have some of the feelings I want, and therefore a rating of 6 felt right for the home environment category.

On the other hand, when I listed out the characteristics I wanted to feel in my love/relationships category, versus where I am today, I scored myself much lower at 1. I scored my career/

calling category at 5 and my travel category at 8.

Doing some free writing about each category in your journal can have additional benefits. It can help you understand what's working and what isn't, especially if it is a complicated category. When I journaled about my home environment category, my kitchen rose front and center in my mind. Suddenly, I realized how important my kitchen was to me. In my last apartment, I had a pretend kitchen, and my current apartment needed a serious renovation. But size wasn't everything. In Minnesota, I had a huge kitchen, but I no longer wanted all that space. Letting myself free write in my journal about my home helped me see exactly what was important to me in a kitchen: good counter space, a place to sit and have coffee, a place for my cookbooks, and good, simple appliances.

So, if you get stuck, open yourself up to free writing about any complicated categories, and I promise you, you'll then be able to expand and feel all the emotions you might be holding inside.

Now it's your turn. Spend time looking at your category descriptions in your journal and on your vision board, then for each category, write on the chart in your journal how you feel today.

Now give each of your categories a *today* rating of where you are right now. Here is what mine looked like:

Category	Rating
Home Environment	6
Travel	8
Career/Calling	5
Love/Relationships	1

Now you add those ratings into your vision board graph.

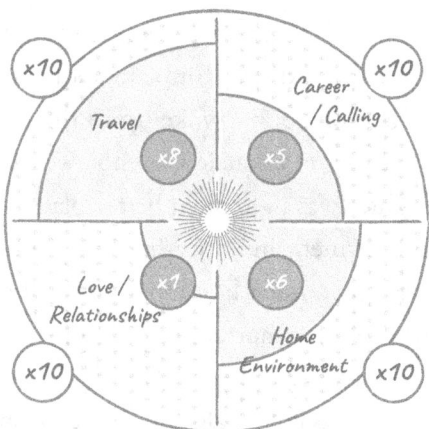

You can now visualize the gaps between where you are now and where you want to be.

In the next chapter, we'll start to create ways to slowly close that gap, but, just like when we order an Uber, we have to acknowledge where we are to begin the journey to where we want to go.

Activity 3: Prepare for Twists and Turns

Sometimes things happen that are out of our control and disrupt our next-chapter plans. Instead of letting these changes derail our next-chapter dreams, accepting, right at the outset, that "life happens" will help us pivot when the unexpected happens.

For example, Boston is my home and Paris fuels my imagination, but my children and grandchildren live in Minnesota. Just a year ago, my daughter's life drastically changed, and she needed my help. I had to adjust all my plans, but I still wanted to find a way to move forward with my next-chapter dreams. Initially, I thought all my trips to Minnesota were temporary. For the first couple of months, all I did was complain about the hotel costs I was incurring. Then one day, I woke up to the fact that my life wasn't going to return to what it was, nor would I want it to, because my daughter was in a much better place. So, I bought a tiny, affordable apartment in a fifty-five-plus co-op community in Minnesota that gave me a home base for my monthly trips. My stays in Paris are now shorter, but I go more often, which is actually working out well.

When life throws us curveballs, it's easy to wish things could go back to how they were. But ultimately, we must accept our new reality and adjust our dreams to accommodate it. Whether it's elderly parents, your own health, kids, grandkids, or even economic factors like a downturn in the real estate or stock market, these events are often out of our control. However, we can control how we respond. We don't have to be martyrs or saints, sacrificing our dreams for the next twenty or thirty years because of an event that we have zero control over. Instead, we can get creative and find ways to pivot. I have found that acknowledging those out-of-control situations in advance helps me to avoid crashing when they happen.

Take some time to list the potential challenges or events that could arise as you work toward your next-chapter dreams. You might even want to brainstorm a few possible pivots that could work for you—but really, just acknowledging the possibility of these life surprises can be enough.

4

Mind the Gap

This step is all about how we close the gap between where we are and where we want to be, and we start by examining our habits. How we choose to spend our time each day is typically a long series of habits involving our sleep, eating, work, health, social life, and spiritual life. Consciously, we have goals we want to achieve. Unconsciously, we seek out things that provide us with short-term pleasure or comfort. Between our conscious goals and our subconscious routines, desires, and comforts lie all our habits—both physical and mental. These habits are the magical lever that can take us from where we are to where we want to be.

My Story

At my age, health is at the forefront of my mind. Recently, I took a few blood tests that forced me to get honest with myself. Both my sisters had heart attacks in the past couple of years, and it was time I faced reality and admitted my hidden habit: I have a candy addiction.

If you want to pinpoint a habit that needs changing, a good place to start is looking at the things you do that you don't want the world to see. For me, that's candy. Not chocolate, which at least has some health benefits, but flat-out junk candy. We're talking Good & Plenty, Jelly Bellies, Swedish Fish, licorice, you name it! I love them all. I rarely admit my addiction to anyone, and no one would guess, unless they saw my candy cupboard. Amazon is my accomplice, with its discreet, generic cardboard boxes delivered to both my Paris and Boston apartments. And I can rationalize my habit like you wouldn't believe. For instance, I found a Swedish candy company in Seattle that uses natural ingredients to make their candy. Surely that's healthier, right? Oh, the games we play with ourselves.

I've had intermittent success controlling my addiction in the past. I'd avoid the candy aisle in the grocery store and resist even glancing at the Haribo varieties at the checkout line. But sooner or later, I'd cave, buying "just one" box or bag, and then I'd be back at square one.

There is always a reason behind our unhealthy habits. My addiction started when I was a child growing up in a dysfunctional household. My escape was reading my books and eating candy. The sugar comforted me, while the stories provided an escape. While I had compassion for the roots of my addiction, I knew it was time to stop making excuses. This habit was clearly out of alignment with my next-chapter goals. I want to see my grandkids graduate from college and get married. I want to stay healthy enough to avoid becoming a burden to my two kids. That meant I had to stop lying to myself and deal with my secret habit.

It was a huge obstacle that kept me from living the full next-chapter life I had designed for myself. As the great dancer Ruth St. Denis said, "How in the end can one possibly hold anyone responsible for our underdeveloped visions or undeveloped strength of character?" Whether I put another piece of candy in my mouth was completely within my control, and no one else could close that gap for me but me. (Read further in activity 1 to see how I dealt with this.)

Some of our bad habits are long-standing, like my candy addiction, while others emerge when life throws new stresses at us, and we react in ways that are at odds with our dreams.

This happened to me recently with my daughter. After enduring a heart-wrenching five years of estrangement, she called me, crying but strong, and apologized for how she had treated me. She shared that she had lived through years of escalating abuse from her husband, and her estrangement from me had been one of his demands. A recent horrific incident involving the police finally allowed her to leave him and move, with her six children, into her father's house—my former family home.

That phone call changed everything. I couldn't move back to Minnesota, but I promised to spend one week a month with her, at least for the time being.

It was hard, especially at the beginning. My daughter and her children were struggling with the effects of years of trauma and had left behind all their belongings—clothes, books, toys, even their car. I spent days cleaning my former home, cooking dinners for the entire family (including my ex-husband), listening to painful sharing, and trying to help my daughter navigate her new life.

I wanted to do it all, but I started feeling ungrounded. I was living two lives—one was in Boston and Paris, and the other in my former home during the day while sleeping in a budget hotel. Now retired, my ex was home all the time, and I saw him more than I ever had, even during our marriage. He acted like the past ten years and our excruciating two-plus-year divorce had never transpired. Even stranger, I fell into an old familiar habit. Every night when my daughter took her children upstairs for baths and bed, I'd clean the kitchen, then sit with my ex-husband and listen to his stories with the television blaring sports in the background.

After five months of this, I realized I couldn't keep living this double life. I was in the middle of writing this book, recording weekly YouTube podcasts, and producing content about designing our next chapters, yet I wasn't living in alignment with what I was writing about. At night, I was staying in a cold, cheap hotel room. During the day, I was cleaning my former home, cooking and then sharing dinner every night with my ex-husband, who still spoke poorly of me behind my back. Needless to say, I felt used and vulnerable.

One day, on a long walk along the Charles River in Boston, I realized that I would never return to my former life, where I split each year between Boston and Paris. Much as I loved that life, I cherished time with my daughter and grandchildren even more. Suddenly, I knew I was embarking on yet *another* next chapter, another big transition and, therefore, needed some new habits and routines. That often happens in our next chapters!

It was clear I needed my own space, a place that allowed me to set boundaries and continue working on my dreams while still supporting my daughter.

If I still wanted to write my book and do my weekly podcasts, I'd have to figure out some better habits during my Minnesota weeks. I didn't yet know what the answer was, but I did know that listening to my ex-husband ramble on each evening after cleaning up his kitchen made no sense. I had to have the courage to say goodnight to my daughter and grandkids and leave, even if it meant returning early to an empty hotel room.

This led me to those words of Ruth St. Denis again. What was in my control?

It was obvious. If I was going to continue spending a fourth of my time in Minnesota indefinitely, I needed a space that had some permanence, a place where I could create boundaries around my next-chapter goals and dreams. I needed to find balance during those weeks I was in Minnesota. Plus, I'm a nester who loves pretty spaces, and that hotel made me sad. So, I started looking at apartments, but everything was beyond my budget. As I lamented over a dinner with two old friends, one of them suggested the co-op building where her mother lived. She said it was affordable, safe, and well-managed. Sight unseen, one month later, I purchased a lovely, small one-bedroom apartment in that building.

I now have my own little space, which allows me to support my daughter and even have a grandchild sleepover from time to time. More importantly, the space allows me to continue to pursue and protect my next-chapter dreams. My Paris life also had to change. I no longer spend three months at a time in Paris, but I go for shorter periods and more often. It was all possible once I let go of how I had been living before my daughter reentered my life and embraced new habits for this new next chapter.

I share this story because unexpected things will happen that easily disrupt our next-chapter dreams and goals. We can't control the events themselves, but we can control how we respond. Ultimately, you are the one who decides whether to abandon your next-chapter dreams or find creative ways to close the gap and stay on course toward the life you want.

What Does Your Gap Look Like?

In the previous chapters, you've done the work to envision exactly what you want your fabulous next chapter to look like. You know what you want to be doing, how you want to feel, and how you want to live. You've also been honest with yourself, examining every aspect of your current life and pinpointing exactly where you are right now in comparison to where you want to be.

Addressing and closing the gap between where you want to go and where you are right now comes down to habits. While it may sound tedious, the wonderful thing is that we are in full control of our habits—both visible habits and mental. These habits will ultimately determine whether or not we achieve our goals and dreams. So, let's dive in.

Your Habits

Habits form the operating system inside each of us. They determine what kind of life we live. Something as small as the self-care habit of how often you brush your teeth will determine whether you get cavities. Exercise and eating habits shape how you feel and impact your overall health. Relational habits, such as how much time you allocate to the important relationships in your life, determine the depth and connection of those relationships. Productivity habits determine your career success as well as your ability to move forward on a project you want to complete.

A *habit* is defined as a settled tendency or usual manner of behavior that becomes nearly or completely involuntary. James Clear, the author of the bestseller *Atomic Habits*, calls our habits a "routine or practice performed regularly; an automatic response to a specific situation."

Habits can be mental, physical, or even emotional. You have habits for how you deal with stress, your self-talk, what you eat, how you spend your time, how often you check your phone or browse certain social media platforms, and what you do to relax, treat, and revive yourself. Think of your average day, and you'll see a series of routines that make up your daily habits.

As humans, we like our habits. They become second nature to us, and we don't even have to consciously think about many of them. We drive the same way to work, add the same amount of cream to our coffee, and get ready in the morning using the same routine. In our daily habits, we go through many of the same steps all day, every day. Disrupting a habit can be jarring—like forcing yourself to drive a different way to work, brushing your teeth with your nondominant hand, or exercising in the evening rather than in the morning. Any change to your habits will make you uncomfortable until you've incorporated the new habit into your daily life.

Our habits determine if we achieve our goals or not. As author James Clear says, "Your outcomes are a lagging measure of your habits." If you aren't getting closer to a goal or dream you have, it doesn't mean you need to rewrite the goal, it means you simply need to look at your habits and assess whether they support or sabotage your goals.

You already know how you want to feel in your next chapter. You've identified the categories of your life that you want to focus on for the next year. Now it's time for you to examine the habits of the person you want to become and compare them to the habits you engage in today to see where you need to make changes.

No habit is too small or too insignificant, nor do the steps to change a habit need to be huge. Start easy. Do one thing differently. Real change begins with baby steps.

Activity 1: Identify the Habits That Are Not Serving You

It's time to list the habits that aren't taking you where you want to go. If you are uncertain where to start, go back to your vision board and focus on the feelings you want to experience in each category you have on your board. Then ask yourself what habits you currently have that don't support those feelings in your next chapter. Remember, no habit is too small or insignificant. Habits are what will determine the life you live in your next chapter.

Furthering the example of my candy addiction, my afternoon double espresso was always accompanied by something sweet. I'd start with one piece of candy and soon it became many pieces. The sugar high eventually became a more important habit than the caffeine hit. One of my next-chapter goals was to be healthier, and that meant I had to cut out junk sugar. The afternoon candy binge didn't align with the woman I wanted to be in my next chapter.

Simply eliminating the candy from this afternoon espresso habit was too big of a shift. When I examined it more closely, I realized my espresso and candy routine provided me with two key feelings I craved in the middle of my day: *energy and pleasure!*

This is the first step to changing our habits: understanding what they are delivering for us.

Consider your next-chapter categories, then take your journal and write out:

Habit that doesn't align with my goals	The feelings this habit gives me

Activity 2: Brainstorm New Habits to Deliver Similar Feelings

Eliminating candy and espresso never worked for me in the long run because I hadn't found a new habit that was as soothing and enjoyable, while still delivering the *energy* and *pleasure* I wanted. So, I started experimenting. First, I tried black tea with honey. Incredibly boring. Then I skipped my afternoon espresso altogether, but that felt punitive—and I still craved caffeine. Finally, I remembered something my father had introduced me to: green tea. He had developed a love of green tea when he was stationed in Japan in the 1950s, and one of his retirement rituals was to make a pot of green tea along with a small bowl of popcorn each afternoon. I loved joining him for this ritual when I visited him.

Now, around 3:00 p.m. each day, I make myself a matcha tea latte. It's a little sweet because I use oat milk, but the matcha (powdered green tea) offers a healthy dose of caffeine without the sugar overload from candy. I even get to use my fun, twirly handheld mixer to froth the latte. I add a dash of maple syrup into my oat milk, along with the matcha, which is even recommended by Dr. Andrew Weil. This new ritual has become even more soothing and enjoyable than my old espresso and candy routine. Plus, it feels really good to create a habit that aligns with my next-chapter goals.

Now it's your turn. Think of some new habits you can create that deliver some of the same feelings as the habits that no longer support your next-chapter dreams.

Feelings I get from my current habit	New habit aligned with my goals that could deliver those same feelings

Activity 3: Chart Your Time

Time is the most precious commodity we have, and it's the same for everyone. Not even the wealthiest among us can buy more than twenty-four hours a day, seven days a week, or 365 days a year. Identifying how you choose to spend your time can be one of the most critical steps to recognizing habits that are sabotaging your goals and desires.

A time log is a tool for observing how you're spending your most precious and valuable resource. Track everything in your time log: sleeping, eating, cooking, driving, socializing, working, journaling, writing, painting, researching, and of course your time spent on the internet and social media. Be as detailed and exact as possible.

The more precise you are, the easier it will be for you to analyze how you are spending your 168 hours each week. This will help you identify what habits need to change or improve if you are going to live that fabulous next chapter you've envisioned on your vision board.

Are you spending too much time on social media? Are you spending time with people out of obligation rather than enjoyment? Are you getting enough sleep? Are you nourishing your body with healthy, well-planned meals? Are you building in enough time to refuel so that you have the energy to create what you want to create?

Examining how you spend your time can make a huge difference in the habits you adopt to close the gap between where you are and where you want to be in your next chapter. Go to your journal or next-chapter workbook and create a weekly chart and track your time.

Weekly Time	Mon	Tues	Wed	Thurs	Fri	Sat	Sun
12:00 am							
1:00 am							
2:00 am							
3:00 am							
4:00 am							
5:00 am							
6:00 am							
7:00 am							
8:00 am							
9:00 am							
10:00 am							
11:00 am							
12:00 pm							
1:00 pm							
2:00 pm							
3:00 pm							
4:00 pm							
5:00 pm							
6:00 pm							
7:00 pm							
8:00 pm							
9:00 pm							
10:00 pm							
11:00 pm							

Fill in your time chart for at least four days, or better yet, a week. You can use this time log whenever you are feeling overwhelmed and want to explore what is going on with your time. Then make note of all you learned. Are there any surprises in how you are spending your time? How do you feel about the time you are giving to each part of your life?

Remember my story about sitting with my ex-husband after cleaning up his kitchen? Not a good use of my time—just an old habit. That was glaringly visible when I did my own time log. Write down what you observe.

Next, write down any changes you want to make to how you spend your time: what you'd like to decrease or increase, omit or add.

Changes I'd like to make to my time expenditure

Activity 4: Chart Your Mindset

The next important habit to explore is your *mindset*, or what is going on in your head. Your inner voice is speaking to you all the time, giving you moment-by-moment feedback about how you're doing, and it also creates stories from your past that shape your identity and self-image. These stories are on repeat in your mind and become the foundation of all your habits.

For example, if you like to say, "I'm a night owl, not a morning person," you'll create habits that support that story. You'll put off doing things until the evening, maybe drink caffeine at 6:00 p.m. to stay alert, and look forward to all the things you plan to do at night. Naturally, you'll then have trouble waking up in the morning! Your story—"I'm a night owl"—gives you permission to create all sorts of habits that align with that narrative.

But what if you switched it up? What if you told yourself, "I'm a morning person. I do my best work before noon. I love getting things done early so I can slow down later in the day." Now you are setting the stage to create habits that support this new story.

Start by identifying the stories you tell yourself about who you are. Some examples include:

- I hate mornings
- I'm a good partner
- I almost always eat heathy foods
- I'm a good cook
- I love to entertain
- I am too busy
- I never have time to do what I want
- I have to take care of others first
- I'm a bad writer or communicator
- I'm no good with money
- I'm a sugar addict
- I don't know which clothes look good on me

The stories and beliefs I hold about myself: I am a person who . . .

Now that you've identified some of your stories, write down the habits you engage in that support those statements. If you "hate mornings," maybe you hit the snooze button til 9:00 a.m. If you're a "bad writer," maybe you put off any writing task until the last minute. If you're "a good partner," maybe you spend the evening catching up with your spouse, even though you'd prefer to take time to journal because that helps you unwind and prepare for the next day.

In this exercise, you're uncovering the habits that support any negative stories you have created about yourself.

My old story: I am a person who . . .	The accompanying habit that supports this story

You know how you want to feel in your next chapter, so now is the time to come up with a new story that fits the next chapter you desire. Then brainstorm a few habits that might support those stories. For instance:

Old story: *I'm bad with money.*

Habits may include: Never looking at my checking account, having no clear understanding of how much I'm spending or what I'm spending it on.

New story: *I'm great with money.*

Habits may include: Tracking expenditures each day/week, becoming aware of where my money is going, and being intentional about my spending, which allows me to transfer any surplus into a "fun" account just for excursions and self-pampering.

Old story: *I have to put others first.*

Habits may include: Checking on my adult kids or elderly parents first thing every morning.

New story: *I care for myself first and then have more to give.*

Habits may include: Exercising and meditating for one hour each morning before checking in with family.

Now you try it!

New story aligned with my next-chapter dreams	New habits that support this new story

Our habits determine how we will close the gap between where we are and where we want to be. Remember to start small. You want your new habits to be as enjoyable and comfortable as the habits you are replacing. We naturally seek comfort, security, and things that feel good, so apply those same qualities to your new habit. I want you to enjoy every little baby step you take as you close your gap!

Every time you perform one of these new habits, remind yourself of your new story, whatever that is. Over time, these habits will become second nature, and the old story will fade away.

Step

5

Try On Those Next-Chapter Ideas!

You have an idea—or maybe several—of what you want to accomplish in the next year. Now it's time to explore further, to jump in and begin to try your ideas on. What exactly do I mean by this?

Think of it like shopping for an outfit for a special occasion. You have a vague idea of what you want—a midi-length dress with a V-neck, comfortable but elegant shoes, a handbag that's both practical and chic. You know your size, your favorite colors, and which brands suit you. But even with all that knowledge, you'll have a much better chance of looking and feeling fabulous if you head to the dressing room first and try on a variety of options.

It's the same with your next-chapter dreams. You have a solid idea of what you want to create in this phase of your life. You are fairly clear on how you want to live and what is most important to you. And just like in that dressing room, it's time to try on those ideas—experimenting with different options to find the best fit for your next chapter.

My Story

One of my American expat friends living in Paris had started an online magazine for women that focused on France. For years she encouraged me to launch my own magazine, offering her team to publish it. As a coach, with a specialized client base of executive women, I wasn't convinced I'd have enough of an audience to support a magazine, so I resisted her intriguing idea.

Instead of jumping straight into publishing, I decided to test the waters. I asked if I could create a section in her magazine called "Conversations with an Entrepreneur," where I would interview female entrepreneurs in Paris. She agreed.

I interviewed, photographed, and wrote several articles for her magazine and discovered that I loved interviewing women and writing about their entrepreneurial journeys. It wasn't a big surprise, given my long-standing interest in the choices people make to pursue their dreams—something that makes me a great coach.

Then COVID hit. During lockdown, I was living alone in my newly renovated home in Minneapolis, bored out of my mind, and baking up a storm. After delivering yet another chocolate mousse and batch of brownies to my son's home, I realized something had to change. During one of my many long phone calls with my magazine friend, I finally decided to give starting my own magazine a try, trusting her team to publish it. In retrospect, it was an impulsive decision—driven partly by the stress of lockdown—but didn't we all go a little batty during COVID? Still, at least I was trying on my dream! I even reached out to Carrie Green, who runs the successful Female Entrepreneur Association and had her own magazine. I learned that she had paused her magazine because it "didn't attract enough readers given the time and expense involved." But, I was determined and refused to believe it! I was convinced my idea was brilliant, even though Carrie knew the industry and had launched one of the first and most successful membership sites for women entrepreneurs. If anyone knew this territory, she did. I'm embarrassed to say that, in my zeal, I thought I knew better.

In April 2021, I launched *The Real You Magazine*. After

two issues, I realized the name didn't fit, so I changed it to *Extraordinary Women Magazine*. The magazine was aimed at women fifty-plus who had started something new in their next chapters—many were side businesses. Most of the women I interviewed were in France, but I also featured several from the UK and the States. I loved everything about the magazine, but it was expensive to produce. We kept tweaking it—changing cover styles, adding coaching tips, writing how-to articles and broader lifestyle content, and featuring product suggestions from France. But after two years, the magazine still wasn't profitable.

Eventually, I made the tough decision to change my team. It was a courageous move, but my final attempt to try on a new approach. I found a fantastic US publisher, Jen DeVore Richter, who is still my business coach to this day. Trying on different ideas connected me with amazing people. Jen and her team, who were already producing several profitable magazines, had many ideas we could try on to make the *Extraordinary Women Magazine* work. We had bi-weekly calls, which were incredibly beneficial and new for me. Despite all these efforts, we still weren't reaching enough readers or making a profit.

In retrospect, I realize the problem was that I hadn't built up enough of a brand around the topic the magazine was focused on. My coaching clients were executive women who, while interested in a "someday" next chapter, weren't likely to buy a magazine focused on just that. They were used to personalized coaching, not general inspiration. If I had built a larger community or offered group coaching, I might have had a bigger following that could have made the magazine successful. Additionally, my website and social media still focused on career coaching, which didn't position me as a credible magazine publisher or expert in next-chapter design for women. I was like the woman who is convinced she needs a knit dress for the occasion even though it doesn't fit her body type!

Despite these challenges, I met incredible women through the process, many of whom became close friends. These connections taught me that women were hungry for ideas on how to design their next chapter, but they wanted more than quarterly inspiration. I had already been using aspects of my seven-step framework in my coaching, but the magazine didn't allow for that kind of structure. I realized that women wanted a step-by-step process for creating their own next chapters, not just to read about someone else's.

I ran a few informal focus groups and confirmed that women were looking for a way to figure out what they wanted and how to close the gap between their current lives and their dream futures. This realization sparked my creativity, and I solidified the idea for this seven-step framework.

You might think the magazine venture was a total failure, but I learned so much in those three years. I also launched a podcast around the same time, which also went through name changes and multiple platforms. I had no idea what I was doing and neither did the person I had hired to help me. I can laugh about it now, but starting a podcast is hard work, and you don't get good at it overnight. I've heard it said you won't have a good podcast until episode 100!

My divorce and family issues had decimated my self-confidence, but trying on different approaches when launching the podcast and magazine helped me to rebuild it. I had to get honest about what suited my lifestyle and what I enjoyed. Today, I feel completely different about myself, my business, and my relationships because of what I tried on, failed at, and eventually succeeded in creating.

The podcast is now in its fifth year, and I still enjoy it. Moving it to YouTube, as my coach, Jen, suggested, made a huge difference and exponentially grew my audience. So don't give up. You might have to try on several different versions of what you want before you find what feels right.

As much as I loved podcasting, I missed writing after I put the magazine on the shelf. It was only after years of experimenting, adjusting, and trying again that the idea of writing a book finally clicked. After two decades of coaching and refining my seven-step process, I decided to put it all into this book—and now it is in your hands!

And the best part is, *if I can do it, so can you.*

Time to Take Action

You've identified the passions and dreams that matter most to you. You've adopted new habits and routines that are aligned with that next chapter you want. Now it's time to try on all those ideas, and this means jumping in and taking action. Some part of you might balk at the idea. Keep journaling and exploring because it's fun to dream and talk about what you could do. Trust me, I've been there! But remember: the clock is ticking and your "someday" is now.

Activity 1: Try On Ideas for a Vision Board Goal

Take a look at the top four categories you have placed on your vision board. These are your priorities for the next year, so make them your focus. Remember, you are planning for just *one* year.

Here's an example from Samantha, one of my coaching clients. On her vision board, under self-care/fitness, her goal was to eat healthier and exercise more consistently. These are the steps she took to try on her ideas:

A Healthy, Sustainable Eating Program	Ideas to Try On	Thoughts/Benefits/Questions
Healthy meal delivery service	Blue Apron Factor HelloFresh	• Portion control. • Less food waste. • Would I miss cooking creatively? (Or is that an excuse?) • Ask friends who use these. • Affordability? • Try for thirty days, then decide.
DIY meal planning with recipes from expert chefs	Dr. Weil Kris Carr	• I'd enjoy the cooking. • Am I disciplined enough to do this every day? • Try a combo of meal delivery and chef recipes?
Nutritional blogs/vlogs	Ilana Muhlstein Rachel Mansfield	• Follow both on Instagram. • Try a recipe from each to see how easy and tasty it is. • Ask my healthy friends who they follow.

Exercise/ Fitness	Ideas to Try On	Thoughts/Benefits/Questions
Join an exercise-only club	Orangetheory Fitness Life Time Fitness A local yoga studio	• Does signing up for classes help me to stick to it? • Can I take a trial class? • Sign up for trial membership and cancel if I don't like it? • Are there people my age and current fitness level?
Join a club that has benefits beyond exercise	A local athletic club A private club with social benefits and athletics A wellness center with classes and events YMCA	• Take a trial class. • Will I use the club's offerings outside of exercising? • Does creating a community around exercise help me stay consistent? • Check out a wide array of options and costs. • Who belongs to those clubs? Are members my kind of people? Ask a club rep about demographics. • Do I have any friends that belong to any of these clubs? • Create a list of costs and benefits of each.
Invite fit friends to coffee to find out their exercise schedules	Kayla Jenny	• Take notes so I don't forget. • Get their reviews of any clubs they frequent or online workouts they use. • Ask how much effort it really takes to stay fit. Get realistic feedback. • Maybe one is interested in becoming my fitness buddy?

Samantha discovered that she stayed more consistent with exercise when she had accountability—whether from friends, a trainer, or a class. She noticed how much more she enjoyed the exercise experiences if she worked out with friends. "I'll never forget an exercise class I signed up for with a couple of friends, which had us laughing hysterically as we danced around the room, feeling like young girls."

You can see how Samantha explored her options with specific questions in mind instead of quickly signing up for programs, only to find they weren't the right fit because she hadn't done enough research.

Samantha explored feeling enjoyment in both eating healthy and exercising. She knew that if it felt punitive, she'd quit. There is a powerful connection between our goals and our feelings that we should never ignore.

Now it's your turn. Take one category from your vision board and list out the ideas you want to try on before committing. Remember to consider how you want to feel in this category.

Category	Ideas to Try On	Thoughts/Benefits/Questions

Activity 1B: Try On Ideas for Creating a Business

If you're considering starting a business, the steps may be more complex. Here is an example of how to do this activity if you are interested in pursuing a business idea. (If you're not trying to start a business, feel free to skip ahead to activity 2.)

Taylor wanted to transition from a corporate career to a flower arranging business for events other than weddings.

Because she had worked in corporate, she had many professional contacts. She also wanted to explore residential opportunities, such as holiday decorating or even tablescapes for dinner parties, which she had spent years perfecting in her own personal life. She had already done several pro bono flower arrangements for nonprofits, but she knew she had much to learn before officially launching a new business.

Taylor was very clear that she didn't want a brick-and-mortar shop or to focus on weddings. Getting clear on what you don't want so you can focus on what you do can be very helpful.

You'll also need to consider start-up costs. Some businesses have upfront costs such as inventory or needed trainings. Besides start-up costs, there may be ongoing expenses to maintain the business. Taylor didn't want a brick-and-mortar shop for several reasons, especially the ongoing expense of rent, but she still had to think about storage and shipping costs. Do you need to hire any help or assistants?

This leads to the next *big* question of how you will market your business and build credibility. How will people learn about your product or service? When I launched my magazine, I didn't have a big enough following to sustain the costs of producing a magazine, even with me doing all the writing and interviewing. Learn from my mistakes. Make no assumptions that past clients will have any interest in your business, so begin to market yourself as a leader in whatever industry or arena you are pursuing *before* you launch your new product or service.

Besides your credibility in a role, don't forget to do your market research to see if there's enough demand for what you want to do. Are there enough people who want what you are selling?

Market research is important before you launch, because

there is nothing more joy-depleting than trying to make your great business idea profitable year after year.

Just like every other category from your vision board that you are going to try on, you will start by talking with people. Seek out people in the industry you are pursuing. They don't have to be doing the exact same thing, in fact most people will not open their resources to you if you're going to end up their direct competitor. But whether it is selling hand-knit scarves, offering tours to Scotland, or becoming a life coach, talk to people who have been doing something similar. One question will lead to another, and from there, you'll have a clearer picture of what it is you want to create and how to do it.

I've taken a few of Taylor's notes to show you how she strategized her connections:

People in Industry	Connection/ Business	Questions/Notes
Leslie J.	Owns a very successful flower and gift shop close to my home.	• She also does events and weddings • Sourcing flowers • Favorite materials • Her journey, future goals
Cordelia A.	Flower photographer I met on a tour to France. I fell in love with her books.	• Tips for taking beautiful photos • Sourcing flowers • Favorite sources for containers
Terri S.	Longtime corporate event planner, the sister of my good friend Mary.	• How she got in the business • Biggest challenges • Are flowers important?

Lindsay D.	Independent event planner for non-profits; I met her through my work with the symphony.	• Are flowers important in this niche? • Could there be a donation that leads to business? How could I loop that in?

And remember, credibility is key. To sell anything today—a book, coaching, artwork, an organizing service, flower arranging, photography—you have to create credibility in that space. And to do that, you need to build a following as an expert in that area, and social media is one of the best places to accomplish that. For those of you who are cringing with discomfort, I get it. It took me forever to accept this. I'm no social media guru, and yet, I have to use social media and so do you.

There are other ways to promote your business. You might be great at speaking and want to start sharing what you do at women's groups, clubs, neighborhood gatherings, or alumnae groups. You won't be paid for these appearances, but you'll be getting your name out there. It's like the baker who wants to create custom baskets for corporate and special events and starts at the farmers' market, one customer at a time, or makes up complimentary baskets and drops them off at corporate offices.

You'll need some kind of online presence to create credibility, and social media is the easiest way to do that. You don't even need a website in the beginning, but you do need an Instagram page. Think about it. If you see something cool at a neighborhood market, you'll go check out their online presence. Instagram is the cheapest way to create a sense of credibility. And lots can be learned from an Instagram page: Is it is real company? Does it have real products? Is there a link to purchase products? What is the feel of the page? Does it fit with your needs?

Here are some of Taylor's flower business marketing ideas:

Ways to Build My Reputation as an Expert	Where/Contacts/ Questions	Preparations
Instagram	Who is doing this? Flowers are so location specific. Will social media matter, or is it needed to build credibility?	• Need great photos. Could be a credibility tool. Could I use Instagram almost like a portfolio of my work?
Facebook	Are there groups near me that would be interested in my services?	• Photos, possibly business card, maybe have a presentation prepared.
Corporate	Make a list of possible corporate contacts for events/ gatherings to explore opportunities. Contact each and offer to stop by their offices; bring an arrangement. Different department, but does the office purchase flower arrangements for lobbies or welcome desks?	• Business card with photos, pamphlet? • Will need my brand logo and colors: simple but elegant. • Will need small arrangement ideas that are easily put together and display my brand look. • Have my presentation pitch ready for each.

Neighborhood groups	Especially during the holidays, I could do presentations on how to decorate; might lead to hiring me to do their homes.	• How-to workshops: how to make a wreath, how to do table flowers, front entry bouquet, decorating areas of house for holidays. • Do I want to do exteriors or stick to wreaths? • Cards, photos, slide show?
Holiday houses, real estate tours, artisan tours, etc.	Are there any seasonal tours where I could do flower arrangements that would be displayed in the spaces? Possible advertising.	• Make list. • Talk to real estate agents.
Shops	Some shops have floral arrangements. Ask if I could make a few and have my card displayed.	• Do I need to do a couple pro bono? Need a card to put on display.

You can see that trying on a business idea is quite complex, but it is all about trying on *all* the components, not just picking your favorites or choosing those that are most comfortable.

Your business dream-to-reality plan is basically to know what you are selling, determine whether there's a market for it, create a plan of how you are going to let your potential customers know about it, and last, determine if the business has the possibility to make money. The only way you can answer those questions is to begin trying on *all* the business exploration ideas you have.

Following are some templates to follow to begin your exploration. Use your workbook or journal to brainstorm ideas for how to try on all your business ideas. Complete one for each business idea you want to try on.

BUSINESS IDEA		
What Is It?	**What Problem or Need Does It Solve?**	**Who Are the Perfect Clients?**
People in Industry	**Connection/Business**	**Questions/ Notes**
Ways to Build My Reputation as an Expert	**Where/Contacts/ Questions**	**Preparations**

THE PRODUCT/SERVICE I WANT TO CREATE	
Who Is Doing This Too?	**What Is Their Brand All About? Who Is It For?**
What Makes My Product/Service Unique?	**How Could I Communicate That in My Branding?**
My Instagram Page	
The feeling I want my potential customer to feel when they see my branding information	
Colors	

Kinds of photos	
Fonts I love	
My Facebook Page	

Remember: Your first idea is often not your best idea!

Whether it's starting a business or a lifestyle change, so many people learn that their first idea is rarely the idea that succeeds. The big idea, the one that sticks, is often one they didn't even think of until they tried on a few different versions and adjusted their plans based on trial-and-error and what they learned. Recall my journey with the magazine and how that led to a YouTube channel, a podcast, and finally this book! All that trial-and-error leads perfectly into our next exercise.

Activity 2: Find the Gift in Failure

When we're going after our dreams, failure can be the humongous pink elephant in the room we try to ignore. Many women don't even take the first step in trying to create their dream because they are afraid of failing. But when you try on ideas, you're bound to experience some failure. *That's part of the process!* Remember the example we began this chapter with—that special occasion outfit? You don't buy everything you take into the dressing room! That's exactly how this works.

I want you to feel just as detached from any failures you experience as you design your fabulous next chapter as you are with a skirt or a top that you leave behind in the dressing room.

Oh, it's hard, I know. We are hyper-focused on success. The

algorithms of just about everything in our lives dictate that we are only shown the über successful companies or highly followed people. We are shown only the most viewed Instagram profiles, YouTube creators, and podcasters, only the bestselling authors. It's no wonder that these are the people who become our yardstick for success. But remember two things.

First, we don't really know how many years and pivots those people took before they hit the big time. Check out the former versions of Mel Robbins, Kris Carr, Ina Garten, Julia Childs, Gwyneth Paltrow, and more. Every one of them tried on multiple careers and experiences before they got to where you see them today.

Second, these superstars reside on a very narrow pinnacle of success that most of us don't even want. Not all of us want to be celebrities with a thirty-person team to manage and paparazzi hounding us. There are tons of people who have successfully created amazing next chapters and are thriving in every way who are not necessarily household names. And you could be one of them.

So get comfortable trying, failing, adjusting, and trying again. It's the fastest, most efficient, and most dependable way to get from where you are to your fabulous next chapter.

The key to working with failure is reframing it from a mistake to a lesson, even a gift. Recall my yearslong experience with *Extraordinary Women Magazine*. Were all those steps a mistake? Absolutely not. Every step taught me something new, introduced me to new connections, and refined my dream until its final form took shape.

So embrace failure! It's truly research that will lead you to exactly what you want to create in your next chapter. Reflect upon your past failures, write them down, and observe the gifts you've already received from each one:

My "Failure"	What Happened	What Was the Lesson/Gift?

One last thing to remember about failure: Value the negative feedback you receive. Remember when Carrie Green told me she couldn't sell enough magazines to cover the costs of publication? I didn't want to listen and that cost me valuable time and money. You don't want to surround yourself with naysayers, but when you get negative feedback from someone you trust, *listen*. If you continually filter out any negativity, it's like going into the dressing room and not looking in the mirror when you try on that dress or skirt!

Activity 3: Strengthen Your Courage Muscle

Midlife is a time of new experiences, new decisions, new choices—and all that newness can be scary. Let's face it, we humans don't crave change. We want consistency and predictability, and trying out your next-chapter dreams bucks both those desired states.

Yet, you picked up this book because you want something more. You are craving something you currently don't have, and you're tired of putting those feelings aside.

Some the wisest words I've said to myself were when I stepped into the role of being my own parent. If you were the parent of yourself, would you tell your child to "Forget those dreams, they're too risky." Or: "Maybe someday, but right now, just be happy with where you are." Of course you wouldn't tell your child either of those soul-crushing responses. And yet, those are often the things we tell ourselves when we start to put our dreams into actions and get a little uncomfortable.

So do work on your fearful thoughts and find ways to strengthen your courage muscle. Here are a few suggestions to help you stay strong and hold true to your next-chapter dreams:

- Go out for coffee with at least one other like-minded woman to chat about your dreams and fears, and share what you are considering in your next chapter. Be vulnerable and talk about those fears. When we share with others about our fears, we normalize and neutralize them. And there is nothing like sharing fears to bring a little levity to a situation.

- Consider hiring a coach. There are a multitude of coaches for all sorts of goals and life stages. I've been a coach for decades, shifting my focus from corporate to higher education to midlife reinvention. You want a coach who specializes in what you need support on. It should be someone whom you feel comfortable with, but also someone strong enough to hold you accountable, a balance that is no easy feat. (I tell every personal trainer I've ever hired: "I'm going to start to engage you in conversation to avoid working out. You must call me out or I'll self-sabotage!") Make sure your coach is strong. Hiring a coach is a big investment in your future, and you'll want someone who is structured and direct enough to hold you accountable, while at the same time able to help you uncover any blocks or sabotaging behaviors.

- Journal. You're probably thinking, *Gosh, Sharri, how much journaling do you want me to do?* The answer is, a lot! Journaling is the quickest, cheapest, easiest way to help you identify your fears and brainstorm ways to address them. Believe it or not, you actually use a different part of your brain when you handwrite versus typing on a keypad.

Fear always follows a big step. It's natural and normal no matter how perfectly you've planned out your next chapter. Addressing how you can deal with your fears in a logical, methodical manner is so important, because it takes the power out of the fears. Here are examples of some of the biggies when it comes to fear:

My Fear	What Can I Do About This Fear?
I'm too old to start a new career.	Find role models of other women who started a career or passion at my age or older. What would it feel like to be a trailblazer?
This dream might cost too much money.	Meet with your financial adviser to find out what amount of money you could allocate to this dream. Are there tax benefits to starting a business? Are there ways to start with a smaller investment?
When I actually try on the dream, I may not like it.	Switch to a mindset of experimentation and trial-and-error. One idea usually leads to another. If this exact dream doesn't fit, perhaps you'll discover a slightly different version.

Now it's your turn. By listing out your fears and identifying possible solutions, you'll make sure that your fears do not covertly sabotage your next-chapter dreams.

My Fear	What Can I Do About This Fear?

Yes, we are working through our fears and thinking through solutions, but remember to also have fun when you try on all your ideas in the dressing room of your next chapter. There is no such thing as failure when you keep an open mind and an attitude of experimentation and learning.

Step

Write Your
Next-Chapter
Plan

Remember the phrase, "Dreams without plans are just wishes"?

You don't want to find yourself ten years from now, sitting somewhere, wondering where the last decade went. What happened to all those dreams, aspirations, and feelings that you highlighted on your vision board?

There is one way to prevent that scenario: Make a concrete plan!

By now, you've tried on different options for each category highlighted on your vision board. You've put aside the ideas that do not fit and zeroed in on those that do. At this stage, you've gained the clarity to get specific on which goals you are going to pursue and which habits you are building to support those goals.

But before we go any further, let's talk about limitations. Be they financial, geographic, physical, or even emotional, we all face limitations in some form. The good news? You can still achieve your desired changes, even with those limitations in place. By acknowledging and understanding your current reality, you can plan more effectively and set yourself up for successfully attaining the next-chapter goals you want.

My Story

Living in Paris was part of my next-chapter plan because it worked so beautifully for me at the time. What I didn't know when I purchased my Paris apartment was that France has some nasty inheritance laws for non-residents, which would essentially give the French government almost half the value of my apartment upon my death. When I found that out, I realized it would be very financially self-indulgent to leave this Paris property reality to my son and daughter. Therefore, Paris isn't a forever plan for me. Most expats who make Europe their forever home have spouses, families, and communities in those countries and have lived, worked, and built lives there. That wasn't my situation, so I had to be flexible and build my part-time Paris life differently from most expats. This limitation means that owning my Paris apartment has an expiration date. At some point I will sell it and explore lovely little hotels that better suit my trips to Paris post-apartment. This is exactly why we write out our plans on our vision boards for one year, not five, and why we create detailed plans for only ninety days at a time.

But how did my next-chapter plan end up with Paris on it? I share this story because, as you've probably already discovered, when you start to try on ideas, one leads to another, and another, and so on.

My divorce took over two years, so I had plenty of time to reflect on what I really wanted moving forward. I had gotten a master's in mental health counseling and planned to move back to Boston after graduation. I realized in those two years that, as interesting as my studies were, I would rather continue my career as a coach than a mental health counselor, but pivot to university students. I needed lightness and less problems, or so I thought.

Shortly after I moved back to Boston, I got a job at Massachusetts Institute of Technology's career center. I loved it. I love education and get jazzed just walking on a university campus. After a year at MIT, I accepted a bigger position at Northeastern University's career center, where I continued working with brilliant engineering students. It was invigorating, rewarding work. I enjoyed helping young people who were on the cusp of their own very big next chapters! I loved teaching and developing new workshops.

Yet something was missing. I could feel it, but I couldn't put my finger on it at the time. As you may have noticed from my stories, I'm a bit of an oddball. I can follow the straight and narrow, plod along the acceptable path for a good while, but then my creativity and curiosity step in. That's when I change careers, move houses, become obsessed with new ideas, enroll in new coursework, or take on a new hobby. That feeling was bubbling up again. I wanted something more.

One day, while commuting to work, I started reading *The President's Hat* by Antoine Laurain. The book follows the hat of French president François Mitterrand, left behind in a café. The hat changes owners, and each person's life changes when they wear the former president's hat. It somehow gives each wearer the confidence to step into the dreams they never before had the courage to pursue. It's a beautiful little book about how confidence, self-image, and plans are entwined. I almost missed my subway stop as I was so engrossed in my reading.

I asked myself, "What if I put that hat on my head? How would I show up differently? Would I finally have the confidence to go after what was missing from my life?" I still held the dream of living part-time in Europe, but was it to remain a dream forever?

Europe had been the setting of every historical fiction novel I'd obsessed over since I was a kid, starting with *A Little Princess* and *Heidi,* then later *Sarah's Key* and *All the Light We Cannot See.* Thinking about living part-time in Europe made me feel excited and energized. I had had enough sadness and loss in my life, and doing what was acceptable to others whose opinions shouldn't matter to me any longer wasn't bringing me joy or excitement.

Well, as the saying goes, there are no coincidences. One evening, I went to the French Library in Boston to hear Jamie Cat Callen talk about her new book, *Ooh La La!* She mentioned a Paris tour she was organizing, and suddenly, I had a way to try on this new next-chapter idea.

Slowly, ideas and questions entered my mind. What if I didn't stay in higher education even though I was well paid and enjoyed working with students? But I admitted to myself that I found higher education administration constricting amid a cliquish group of colleagues with a mindset that I constantly pushed against. Although the students loved me, I didn't quite fit into the cultural structure of higher education. I seemed to have acquired my solid, secure, dream job, yet I wanted something more.

That Ooh La La trip planted the seeds that allowed my next chapter to bloom. I got to try on Paris and became comfortable enough to arrange many subsequent solo trips. I met my now dear friend Poupie Cadolle and got fitted for the bra that changed my life! I met other friends, many of whom I remain close to now.

On those many subsequent solo trips, as I walked the beautiful streets of Paris, I realized I was gearing up for another change but didn't yet know what it would be. I had fallen madly in love with Paris, as many women do. I loved how I felt as a woman in Paris. I started to feel feminine again, and my new bra was a constant reminder—both at home and in Paris. Even if I was the only one who saw it, I could feel the lace against my skin and remember that I was still a feminine woman. Other subtle changes were happening too. I began to pay attention to my makeup, how costume jewelry could bring light to my face, the importance of colors, as well as clothing that wasn't loose and baggy to hide my weight gain. I found accessories and outfits that made me look and feel good. In Paris, I'd sit in cafés and watch people interact, noticing how women dressed and the subtle flirtations of both men and women. I began to read books about French history, and even incorporated French design aesthetics into my apartment interiors. I was having the time of my life. But could I take it one step further and actually live there?

I was in love with more than the physical beauty of Paris. In Paris there is a subtle appreciation for the joy, beauty, and fulfillment of life that made me begin to question how I could bring that joie de vivre back home with me. Did my job really provide all I wanted in my next chapter? Was job security enough? If I wrote a book about my life post-divorce, would it be interesting and joyful or a tiresome book about a woman who continued to follow the rules and boringly just survived?

I started to see myself as someone more complex than just a producer, a doer, that woman who gets things done. Most of us have been caretakers. I'll even be so bold as to call us CEOs of our homes, children, and family schedules. (This is maybe why divorced men tend to remarry quickly—they need another CEO!) We know how to get things done, and sometimes it's hard to turn off that doer's switch long enough to focus in on what we want at this chapter of our lives. My Paris experience gave me the space to realize I really was a creative, a dreamer, a feminine woman who had lots of plans she could make happen for herself if she focused.

Each time I returned to Boston from those many trips to Paris, I continued working hard at my university job as I quietly plotted out yet another next chapter. One winter, I used all my accumulated vacation time and spent three weeks in a rented apartment on Place Dauphine just off the Pont Neuf (the oldest bridge in Paris). It was the next step in trying on the idea of living in Paris part-time. Those three weeks gave me time to test out living like a local.

I took cooking classes at La Cuisine Paris, found favorite cafés, and window shopped. I went to mass at Saint-Sulpice, sat in the Jardin du Luxembourg, and became a regular at Le Hibou café long before it was hip. Every day, I wandered and explored, and each night, I plotted out my next day's journey on a detailed map. I bought groceries in local stores, pulling them back to my rented apartment with my ubiquitous French grocery trolley. Sitting in the cafés, I wondered how it would feel to quit my university job and restart my private coaching business. My well-paid and high-status job provided a level of prestige, even self-confidence, that working for myself would not. If I restarted my coaching practice, I'd have to hustle again rather than commute to the same office each day. But working for myself would allow me to spend even more time in Paris. Did I really want to live part-time in Paris, and if so, how badly?

Back in Boston, I launched a new online career tool for the office, which was incredibly interesting work, but I was antsy. Nothing was feeling right. Finally, I knew it was time to stop dreaming about my next chapter and start doing. It was time to take my dream from my imagination and make it tangible with a plan.

I gave my notice at the university and planned my next step.

For the first time in a long time, it was all up to me! I had finally worked through all my accumulated issues and pain from the divorce, the disownment by my parents, the estrangement from my daughter. Their opinions no longer mattered.

When you sit down to design the next chapter, the plan must reflect actions that support your dreams. It must be based on what *you* want, what *you* can create and build, and not the choices and expectations of others. Be authentically you in every aspect.

It took me several years to figure out what I really wanted and who I really was without all the roles I had played throughout my life—the dutiful daughter, the supportive wife, the loving mother, the star employee. It's not selfish to reconnect with the person you are deep inside and always have been. That inner person is your legacy, the reason you're here on this Earth at this time and place.

The Way into Your Dream: Writing It Down

It's time to put the pen to paper! You've been trying on ideas, and now you have your plan in mind.

You've addressed your fears and are continually working to strengthen your courage muscle. Yes, this entire designing your next chapter takes a boatload of courage. It's super easy to sit around and let another day, another month, another year go by. But how will you feel if you do that? Your time is now, so keep moving forward!

Writing down your next-chapter plan is critical because it makes the intangible tangible. When you see your dreams in writing, they become real. It's no longer just a wish or fantasy; it's something you can work toward every day.

Activity 1: Connect with Twelve-Year-Old You

This is such a powerful exercise for reconnecting with the essence of who you are, beyond the many roles and responsibilities that may have shaped your life. By revisiting that young version of yourself, you get a glimpse of the pure, unfiltered dreams, hopes, and ideas that existed before life's demands shifted your focus.

Writing a letter to your twelve-year-old self is a way to acknowledge the path you've traveled and reassure her that, in this new chapter, you're making space for her dreams too. You can remind her that her curiosity, creativity, and ambitions are still alive within you, and now is the time to honor them.

This is about giving yourself permission to embrace those childhood dreams, even if they've been dormant for a while. Reassure your younger self that you are ready to take steps to fulfill the passions and goals she once held dear, knowing that you now have the wisdom and experience to guide them into reality.

Activity 2: Write Out Your Next-Chapter Thirty-Day Plan

Your vision board is the foundation of your plan. You'll create a plan for each of your top four categories, and instead of making a traditional one-year plan, we're going to break it down into a much more workable ninety-day plan, then further break that into thirty-day blocks. Your thirty-day plan provides the structure needed to make progress toward your next-chapter goals while staying flexible enough to adjust based on how things unfold. The addition of your feedback and results for each action will be invaluable as you continue to tweak and adjust your monthly and weekly plans.

Let's say one of your next-chapter categories on your vision board is health, specifically to get fit, which you've decided includes strength training, endurance building, and increased flexibility. Your thirty-day plan might look something like this:

My Plan for Strength Training, Endurance Building, and Increased Flexibility

Month of the Year	Plan	Action	Results/Feedback
Week 1	Strength training	Get trainer referrals.	*Got two super referrals.*
		Call/email to check availability.	
		Choose a trainer.	*Chose Anna: I like her.*
		Decide days/times to work with trainer and put in my calendar.	*Starting with thirty-minute sessions feels right.*
	Endurance	Try and then decide on whether in gym or outside.	*Outside is nice but inside is more intense. Alternate.*
		Schedule activity and location: put into calendar.	
	Stretching	Try a yoga class.	*I don't like yoga. Found Sam on YouTube and like her stretching routine.*

		Is there a certain time of day that works best for my body?	*Late afternoons are much better and I get a second wind.*
		Put my stretching schedule into my calendar.	
Week 2	Strength training	Working with Anna two days/week for thirty minutes.	*Not ready for longer sessions. Still tired after thirty minutes.*
	Endurance	Walking on treadmill, biking, swimming twice a week.	*Can't get the courage to get into a swimsuit yet, but walking outside given good weather.*
	Stretching	Stretch at least three times a week.	*Continue stretching with Sam, but also going to check out a stretching class at the club.*
Week 3	Strength	Keep to the same schedule.	*Try a couple of the exercises on my own on off days, especially with the bands.*
		Write down the exercises to begin to prepare myself to add a day without a trainer.	
	Endurance	Whatever I choose, keep up my schedule of three times a week.	*Not ready for longer yet, but when in a gym, variety keeps me from getting bored.*
		Consider adding both variety and length of time.	*I like to do ten minutes on rower, treadmill, and then bike.*

	Stretching	Have a little routine set up for myself that I can do from anywhere three times a week.	*Sam is easiest to plug in when my schedule is busy or traveling. Class gave me ideas for different stretches.*

You can see how the plan is broken down week by week. You could go a little further, and probably will in your calendar, entering the specifics day by day: what day you will meet with the trainer, what days you will walk or work out at the gym, and more. Keep reminding yourself to get as detailed as possible.

The results and feedback section is all about your feedback as you work through each week. Record how you feel, what's worrying you, what you're not ready for, what you like best, how something is benefiting you, and so forth.

This is an invaluable step. Not only will you then have the needed feedback to know what to tweak or replace, but you will also start getting ideas for how this plan might evolve in the future. In the health example, it might mean that you eventually only work with the strength trainer once a week because you've got a good routine that you can do at home. If you worked through your self-conscious fears about getting into the swimming pool, you might realize you need a buddy to join you in a water aerobics class, so finding that person will go on your next week plan. Walking outside might involve getting more intense by trying out hills or a faster pace to see how that feels and whether you want to continue to alternate with inside exercises. The results and feedback part of this activity is what will ensure that you don't abandon your goals because they are uncomfortable. That is when fear wins, and you're beyond that now!

You'll find that the subsequent plans for months two and three will be much less detailed than month one. The results and feedback you provide from month one will inform what goes into the next month's plan. Maybe you didn't enjoy yoga, so it won't show up in the next month's plan. At the end of each week, you are ready to add another week, so you are always creating detailed plans for the next thirty days. For example, if you are always planning out for four weeks, you'll be planning the first week in June as you complete the first week in May.

What's important is that when you complete each thirty-day period, you take a look back at the last thirty days to inform your plan for the upcoming thirty days. After you look back, you'll then adjust your sixty-day plan if needed, and you'll be ready to go out another thirty days so that you always have a ninety-day plan in front of you.

This detailed approach to planning encourages continuous adaptation and feedback, ensuring that your goals remain attainable and enjoyable rather than rigid or overwhelming. By breaking down the plan week by week, and eventually day by day, you're setting yourself up for sustainable progress.

You also want to be sure to consider upcoming events in your schedule that may impact your plan. For example, I don't have a trainer or a gym in Paris or Minneapolis, so I need to have routines set up that I can do from home, *and* I need to be much more self-motivated in those locales. I need to pay attention to how motivated I remain without any accountability and put that into my results feedback. If I start to let my program fall apart without a trainer, it would be an opportunity to find ways to insert more accountability into the plan for the next trip away from home. That could include an online session with my current trainer in Boston to get me back on schedule. It could be regular email check-ins with my current trainer to update her on my progress. I might need to find a buddy to exercise with in the cities I visit away from home. Do I need a gym option, could I purchase access to a hotel gym, and so forth.

Continuing with my example, if I were going to Paris in week 4 of March, it might look something like this:

March	Plan	Action	Results/ Feedback
Week 4 **IN PARIS**	Strength training	Bring bands and have routine in place since no trainer.	
	Endurance	Set up walks in the city: Jardin des Tuileries Notre Dame Jardin du Luxembourg	
	Stretching	Continue with Sam on YouTube.	

Use your workbook for more detailed templates for ninety-day and thirty-day plans. But start with the following guide in this condensed form to make sure you've got a running start. Take just one of your goals from your vision board and make a thirty-day plan for it.

My Plan for _____

[Month]	Plan	Action	Results/ Feedback
Week 1			
Week 2			
Week 3			
Week 4			

Notice how every step of this seven-step process builds on the previous one. Your priorities end up on your vision board and from there, you examine the gaps between where you are now and where you want to be. You start identifying the habits that will take you one tiny step closer to your goal each day. These habits will likely show up in your thirty-day plan for your next three months. Along the way, you'll uncover the fears that crop up as you start living the beginning stages of your next chapter and have some ideas as to how you can overcome those fears. Those fear solution actions can also be incorporated into your thirty-day plan!

Remember, for any goal to be achievable, it must be realistic, clear, and measurable. That's why your thirty-day plan should be as specific as possible. Then, as you try out each action, tweak it based on how you feel and what's working. This step is fluid and constantly evolving because it's tailored specifically to your lifestyle, desires, and responses. That's the plan's superpower: It's built for one person—you!

Your Support Team

Support—we all need it. No one achieves their next-chapter dreams alone. Your support team can make all the difference in your ability to create the next chapter you want. Some people on your team will be cheerleaders, some will be truth tellers, and others will hold you accountable. They can be friends, mentors, spiritual leaders, or former colleagues. My close friends make up my primary support team, and one of them always steps forward when I need a dose of reality.

Sometimes I get so convinced I know exactly what is going on, only to realize I'm wrong. That's where good friends or other members of your support team come in. They help you see clearly when your thinking becomes foggy.

If you're in a relationship, take time to sit down with your partner and have meaningful discussions about what you both want in your next chapters. Partnerships evolve, and this next chapter is a big one for both of you. With the kids grown and possibly retirement on the horizon, you'll likely be spending more time together than ever before. If you are excited to learn more about each other in this stage of life and do the work to support one another's next-chapter dreams, there is a strong possibility they will all come true.

For many years, I knew my husband was incapable of truly loving me. I only found the courage to seek a divorce when I realized what my next chapter would look like if I didn't make a change. Hopefully, not everyone will have such a painful realization, but for some, that difficult choice may be necessary.

If you're not partnered, lean into the support of a good friend, coach, or trusted family member—whoever is a part of your support team. Just make sure they are worthy of your trust and honesty.

Go After Your Next-Chapter Dreams with Love

Remember, planning out your next-chapter dream is not about finding a Band-Aid for an unfulfilling life. Band-Aids don't last, and when they fall off, the wound underneath is exposed.

Your next chapter should focus on using your natural gifts, talents, and interests. We are all born with unique abilities, and throughout our lives, we've gained valuable experience and wisdom. Now is the time for you to ask yourself: How am I going to use my gifts and my experience to leave an imprint on my world?

When you surround your dreams with love and believe in the possibilities of your next chapter, you will make big things happen.

Step

7

Create Your Manifesto!

Congratulations! You made it to the last step! I imagine that so much has changed in your life throughout this process, as it has in mine! This journey has guided you through your next-chapter framework, and you've now got a detailed vision of what your next chapter can be. I hope you're filled with anticipation, excitement, and even joy as you've begun shifting routines and implementing some of the big changes you've mapped out. You've been trying on options and refining your next-chapter design.

This next chapter of your life, like many before, will also contain several mini-chapters. What do I mean by mini-chapters? Well, we all have those major life chapters that mark significant milestones—becoming an adult, building a career, finding a partner, perhaps raising children, experiencing an empty nest, and eventually retirement. Other major chapters may include the loss of a partner through death or divorce, or facing a major health issue for yourself or a loved one. But within these larger life chapters, there are the mini-chapters—smaller events that lead to minor pivots, fresh perspectives, or new routines.

These mini-chapters can be something like moving to a new home in the same city, deciding to take a class or pursue certification in an area of interest, or offering short-term assistance to a family member. These mini-chapters require small adjustments in your routines, and they, too, can leave you feeling off-kilter or ungrounded. Even something as seemingly minor as giving up your afternoon coffee can shake things up for a few days!

Whether it's a mini-chapter or a life-shifting, turn-the-page next chapter that is shaking up your world, it's up to you to decide how you respond. When the proverbial shit hits the fan, you can either fall apart or get up, brush yourself off, and pull out this seven-step framework once again.

Designing your next-chapter framework isn't a one-and-done experience. These seven steps can be your safety net when you find yourself struggling or off-balance. You can return to them as often as needed to get back on track, no matter what life throws your way. When that happens, simply start at the beginning. I promise you will find comfort in reconnecting with yourself, starting with step 1, and finding your pathway forward. Remember:

1. Dream big.
2. Decide what's most important to you right now. Maybe it's time for a new vision board.
3. Get clear on where you are now.
4. Mind the gap.
5. Try on your next-chapter ideas.
6. Write and fine-tune your next-chapter plan.
7. Update your manifesto!

My Story

Throughout the writing of this book, I've had to step back and revisit this framework several times. My living routine had to change due to my daughter's return into my life. I could no longer go to Paris for extended periods of time. I had to throw out my old schedule and embrace a new one, but I didn't want to completely abandon my life in Paris—the city that, in so many ways, changed my life! When I had decided to live half the year there, my daughter was estranged from me and my heart was broken. Paris healed me and brought light back into my life. I had lost hope that anything would change with my daughter, but thankfully it did. And with that, change was in the air once again.

She left her husband who, unbeknownst to me, was a violent, abusive man who ruled the household. I am so proud of her courage to leave with the children and fight to protect them and herself—no small feat. I welcomed her back into my life with hugs of joy, and I also saw the need to rethink and redesign parts of my next chapter. Then, when my oldest grandchild decided to attend the University of Edinburgh in Scotland, suddenly, there was yet another reason to reevaluate my Paris life. This is a perfect example of a mini-chapter. I had to pivot so I could support my daughter, visit my granddaughter in Scotland, and still honor my own big next-chapter dreams to write this book, build my YouTube channel, and whatever other business ventures I decided to pursue.

Honestly, there were moments over this past year when I wondered why I still had these insane goals in this chapter of my life. But as I walked my own talk and reconnected with my younger self—that woman who always put her dreams on the back shelf for another day—I knew I had to do it differently this time. No matter what chapter we're in, our own goals and dreams matter. If we give up on them, we'll feel a sense of resignation that might even evolve into depression.

And when those challenging events do happen, besides using this seven-step framework, I've developed several additional ways to stay grounded and motivated.

Send yourself cards or letters. It might sound like a crazy idea (and I have many!), but I started writing and mailing letters and postcards to myself. Initially, it was a way to preserve my Paris experiences, but over time, these letters evolved into something more personal and took on the voice of journal entries. Even now, when I struggle with life's challenges, I write myself a letter. Sometimes those letters celebrate small wins and accomplishments. Other times, I work through ideas I have or new habits I want to embrace. Something shifts when we physically write down our feelings and talk to ourselves like a best friend. We send cards to people we care about, so why not ourselves?

Experts say that physically writing engages a different part of the brain than typing on a computer. If that's true, it explains why writing letters to yourself can be an incredibly fun and even a powerful way to journal. You get to keep a meaningful memento while helping yourself move forward through whatever might be creating the current struggles in your life.

I have a special box where I keep all my Paris letters, documenting the healing Paris provided me. The letters began with newsy details about the food and cultural differences, but over time, they became more reflective—describing how I interacted with people, how I felt, and how I gradually started walking, dressing, and living differently. One letter describes a lunch at Brasserie Lipp, capturing everything from the men seated on either side of me—how they acted, what they ordered, how they were dressed, their smiles, what their stories might be—to the feel of the restaurant and how it so perfectly suited me. That letter was a conversation with myself about an experience that might have been easily forgotten. So much of our life experiences happen in moments that are later forgotten. Writing letters to yourself is a way to keep those memories alive. Mailing letters home while you're traveling is especially lovely because you will get to relive your trip when you return, open your letters, and read about your adventures.

Buy some flowers. There's something about flowers—you can't look at one without feeling joy and calmness. Flowers make us smile. Whether you pick them yourself or buy them, place flowers where you can see them and let their beauty soothe you. The author and designer Alexandra Stoddard once said, "We should all view life as a garden." What a lovely idea.

Sing. It doesn't matter if you aren't a great singer—just belt it out! I'm a mediocre singer on a good day, but I love music and find joy in singing. Once, I was having a rough day and singing along with Cher's "You Haven't Seen the Last of Me" from *Burlesque* helped me feel empowered and assured that all things would, once again, be possible. Even Sydnie Christmas's performances on *Britian's Got Talent* can have you jumping off the sofa, ready for more. So, just sing!

Incorporate good, healthy self-care habits into your life. Whether it is meditation, yoga, reading, writing, painting, or prayer, find what centers you and make it a part of your daily routine.

I created a next-chapter manifesto to guide me and remind me to value my next-chapter dreams. A *manifesto* is a written declaration of intentions, motivations, and viewpoints that guide a person, a company, or a cause. For you, it can be the foundation that helps guide you through all your decisions in this next chapter.

One of the major challenges of aging is not valuing ourselves enough to create and live out those dreams we still hold tight to. Don't ever say to yourself, "I'm not worth investing in"—whatever your next-chapter dreams may be.

Remember, there are no perfect next chapters.

There is no right way to do this, and no one's next chapter will look the same as anyone else's. You are special. No one has your unique life experiences or your dreams, so embrace and celebrate the uniqueness of *your* next chapter.

I share this because I made the mistake of not embracing and loving my own uniqueness when I started my next chapter. At first, I spent most of my time with women who were building businesses like me, but when I spent time with women who weren't, I would hide what I was working on. I acted like a chameleon, adapting to the environment rather than celebrating my path.

It took me some time to realize that being different is okay. Though I've felt different much of my adult life, I wasn't fully embracing it. I was dancing around my uniqueness. So don't make my mistake. Spend time with people from various walks of life, share what you are trying to create in your next chapter, and celebrate their uniqueness too! You never know who might want to collaborate with you or has a special skill set you need to help launch your dreams.

As Coco Chanel said, "In order to be irreplaceable, one must always be different." Celebrate the uniqueness that is you.

In a moment I'm going to have you create your own manifesto, but first I'll share mine with you as an example. You can see that it is all written in the first person. Your manifesto is your proclamation to the world!

Sharri's Next-Chapter Manifesto

1.   I will never, ever give up on my dreams!

My dreams are intricately connected to a feeling of hope. I can't have hope without dreams, and I can't have dreams without hope. So, if at any point in my life, I feel any resignation that my dreams don't matter or it's too late for them to happen, it's time to return to step one of designing my next chapter and reconnect to my dreams.

Dreams are what make humans amazing. Without them, there would be no love affairs, no children, no adventures to new places, no new products, no cures for disease, no scientific or technological breakthroughs, no prayer or meditation, and no smiling.

When I need a reminder of this, I watch the documentary *Nothing Left Unsaid* by Anderson Cooper and his mother, Gloria Vanderbilt. Despite all the fame and success, Gloria lived through deep sadness, including the suicide of her son, yet she remained, as Anderson describes, one of the most positive and optimistic people he knew. Even in her nineties, she believed a great love affair was still just around the corner.

As Nelson Mandela said, "There is no passion to be found playing small, in settling for a life that is less than the one you are capable of living." That's why I commit to dreaming—and dreaming big!

2. I will stay forever curious and try to view the world as though I am a child.

I will always strive to see the world through the eyes of a three-year-old full of curiosity. Curiosity sparks the ideas that fuel my dreams and raises the questions: Why not? Who says? What if?

Young children are curious about everything. Just spend time around a three-year-old, and you'll be bombarded with questions like "Where do birds sleep?" or "Why your lips are purple?" As we age, we tend to get comfortable with our routines, and our curiosity about the world dwindles. We eat the same things, go to the same places, and spend time with the same people. Living entirely with our routines can become static, making us less curious.

Instead, I choose to embrace a childlike view of the world and keep asking: Why?

3. I will accept that change happens, and it might be for the good.

Even if I've drawn up the best plan in the world and begun taking steps, I know that things will happen that force me to shift or pivot a little or a lot. Accepting change allows me to stay flexible, not stomp my feet or scream out loud, or worse, give up on my dream whether it's bad news, a market downturn, or a friend or family member in need.

Looking back, I see I often delayed my dreams, thinking I could get to them once I resolved other issues. But just as one thing got fixed, something else would crop up, and the years marched on. Once I accepted that changes and disruptions are inevitable, my mindset shifted. (This is where the seven-step frames helps. It supports working through the impact of changes—big and small.)

4.   I use boundaries to eliminate confusion in my life.

When life feels overwhelming, I check in with my boundaries. Bound-aries are not selfish; they are necessary for everyone. I alone am responsible for setting and maintaining boundaries around my habits, routines, and the people I spend time with.

Raising children is about teaching boundaries—both theirs and ours. Work-life balance is about having and maintaining boundaries. Societies only run well and without chaos when there are societal boundaries that work for the greater good. I've learned that I can't be my best self when I let others trample on my boundaries. It's my responsibility to protect them.

We often overly focus on whether our food is healthy but neglect the toxicity of certain relationships. Toxic people can be just as detrimental to our well-being, if not more. Whether it's a snide friend, a family member with unreciprocated expectations, or a boss stealing your ideas, toxic people love stepping all over boundaries.

If someone is messing with your plans or dreams, it's time to check your boundaries.

5.   I will communicate my feelings (with compassion) and ask for clarification if needed.

Communication is the key to all good relationships, plain and simple. Every failed or strained relationship in my life has happened because of poor or reactive communication: my marriage, my first love, my estranged parents, issues with adult children and their spouses, and even people who I thought were good friends.

Avoiding communication is the easy way out, and it's also the coward's way. It's far more difficult and courageous to express how you feel and ask someone what's bothering them. In the end, open dialogue brings clarity and prevents a multitude of problems.

My family has a difficult legacy of generational estrangement. When I completed a family genogram for my master's program, I discovered a pattern of relational cut-offs, especially on my father's side. When my own parents cut me off after I connected with my son, I realized that for them, cutting people off was easier than dealing with difficult emotions. It's a painful legacy—one I've worked hard to end.

Byron Katie taught me to ask, "What do I know is true?" That question brings clarity when I'm spinning around worst-case scenarios. The truth often lies in observable behaviors. If I really want to know what is behind someone's behavior, I need to communicate and ask for honesty in return.

No one can read your mind. If you don't communicate your dreams, no one can help you realize them. So, sit down with those closest to you and share what you're trying to create in your next chapter. Let them behind the curtain of your mind to see exactly what dreams you are pursuing. That's the only way they can support you on your next-chapter journey.

Activity 1: Create Your Own Next-Chapter Manifesto

Now it's time for you to create your personal manifesto for your next chapter—your guiding motto for navigating the twists and turns of life. This manifesto will be a set of guidelines and reminders written from your wisest self, designed to keep you aligned when you face inevitable challenges or pivotal moments.

1. Find a quiet, comfortable place where you can journal without distraction. Allow yourself a moment to settle in and connect with your inner wisdom.

2. Imagine your wisest self—the version of you who has gained insight through life's ups and downs—coming forward. What advice does she have for you as you step into this new phase? Trust that she knows exactly what you need.

3. Let her voice guide you as you write down anywhere from three to seven rules for living. These may be centered on self-care, nurturing your passions, spiritual beliefs, or key life lessons that you want to carry with you. Think of them as your personalized toolkit for life's challenges—simple yet powerful reminders that will ground and guide you.

4. Don't overthink it! Your wise self knows best. Allow her voice to emerge naturally. Whether it's "trust the timing of my life" or "protect my energy fiercely," write down what feels right.

5. Use my manifesto as inspiration if you need a starting point, but remember this is about you and your unique path.

This activity is about honoring your truth and creating a roadmap for your next chapter, filled with wisdom and intention.

Going Forward

It has been my absolute pleasure and joy to share this journey with you! I hope this seven-step framework has become a valuable tool for helping you understand where you are, where you want to go, and how you'll get there. Remember, you can revisit these chapters and exercises anytime you need to create a new next-chapter plan or refine your current one.

Stay connected and explore more online resources at sharriharmel.com. I'm always here for you—reach out with any questions or requests. I'm cheering you on every step of the way as you design and step into your most fabulous next chapter yet!

Acknowledgments

So many people contributed to what became this book, but first I want to thank you, the reader, for letting me share my very personal stories. Hopefully, you can use them to enrich your own next chapter journeys.

They say people come into our lives when we most need them, and I want to say thank you to the following people who each, in their own way, shifted what I thought was possible in the next chapter of my life.

Poupie Cadolle, my dear Parisian friend, your support and encouragement as we shared our life stories, explored European history, and discussed French culture developed a friendship I will forever cherish. And let's not forget, you created the bra that changed my life, helping me to reconnect with my femininity and embrace a renewed sense of self.

Jen DeVore Richter, the best business coach who not only saved *Extraordinary Women Magazine* but also encouraged me to think bigger and bolder. From launching my YouTube channel to writing this very book, your strategic mind, brilliant advice, and amazing team have transformed the possibilities I see for my next chapter. I'm endlessly grateful for your guidance.

Debbie Ford, through your transformative work on the shadow, you gave me the courage to find my son and face the emotional blocks that had kept me stuck for so long. Your teachings opened doors within me that I never thought possible. I will forever miss your amazing spirit.

To the university students and staff I had the privilege of working with over the years, thank you for welcoming my gifts, for teaching me new lessons in everything from technology to running workshops, and for letting me continually try out so many of my crazy ideas. Playing even a small part in helping the next generation reach their potential was an experience I will forever treasure.

And finally, to all my clients, thank you for trusting me with your most precious dreams and challenges. It has been an honor to work alongside you as we crafted the careers and lives you envisioned. Your journeys continually inspire my own.

With deep gratitude,

Sharri

About the Author

Sharri Harmel is a dynamic force of transformation, guiding others through the pivotal moments of their lives with grace and insight. From her early career as a stockbroker to her roles as a stay-at-home mom, a dedicated volunteer, and later a career and executive coach, Sharri has continually embraced new roles to empower and uplift those around her. Her journey took a significant turn when her twenty-five-year marriage ended, prompting her to apply her accumulated wisdom to redefine her own future.

Sharri is the vibrant creator and host of the Extraordinary Women with Sharri Harmel YouTube channel, where she addresses the myriad of challenges women face as they seek to achieve their dreams. Her channel also features the empowering "Come with Me . . ." series, which takes viewers on imaginative journeys to cities and locations that inspire new possibilities. Sharri also offers personalized coaching to clients seeking tailored guidance and accountability in designing their next chapters.

Through her writing, videos, and coaching, Sharri Harmel continues to be a beacon of inspiration, helping others to embrace change and create lives filled with joy and purpose.

Visit her online at sharriharmel.com.

Your Fabulous Next Chapter Workbook

I'm thrilled you're diving into designing *your* fabulous next chapter!

Here's your next step: grab the free workbook that accompanies this book! Just scan the QR code below, pop in your email address, and I'll send the workbook straight to your inbox. It's packed with all the exercises, activities, and insights you'll need to make the most of this journey.

Feel free to mark up the pages, jot down ideas in your journal, or dive in however feels best for you. This is *your* time—let's make it incredible together!

Personalized Next Chapter Coaching

Ready to take your dreams to the next level?

If you're craving clarity, focus, and a real plan for your next chapter, let's dive in together! Sign up for a *60-minute, one-on-one breakthrough session* with me. In this powerful session, we'll explore your dreams, refine your ideas, and work together to find your focus. We'll set meaningful goals and craft a personalized action plan to bring your vision to life.

This is your moment—let's make it count!